# MASTER
## ADDING & SUBTRACTING
# FRACTIONS
## WORKBOOK

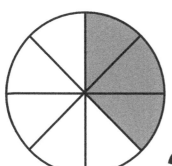

$$\frac{3}{8} + \frac{5}{6} =$$

$$\frac{9}{24} + \frac{20}{24} = \frac{29}{24}$$

## DR. PI SQUARED

Master Adding & Subtracting Fractions Workbook
Dr. Pi Squared

Nonfiction/children's/mathematics/arithmetic
Nonfiction/education/mathematics/arithmetic

ISBN-10: 1463551436
ISBN-13: 978-1463551438

# Contents

# Basic Terminology

An **integer** is a whole number. Each number in the following sequence is an integer:

$$0,1,2,3,4,5,6,7,8,9,10,11,12,13, \ldots$$

A **fraction** is a number that comes between two integers. For example, $\frac{1}{2}, \frac{2}{3}, \frac{4}{7}$, and $\frac{3}{2}$ are all fractions.

You can visually represent an integer as a number of whole pies. For example, the integer 4 is represented below as 4 whole pies.

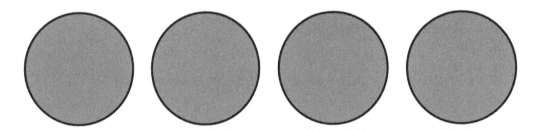

A fraction can't be represented as a whole number of pies, but must be represented with slices of pies. For example, the fraction $\frac{3}{5}$ is illustrated below by dividing a pie into 5 slices and shading 3 of them.

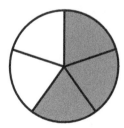

A fraction can be expressed in the following form:

$$\text{fraction} = \frac{\text{numerator}}{\text{denominator}}$$

For example, in the fraction $\frac{3}{4}$, the **numerator** is 3 and the **denominator** is 4.

A fraction is called a **proper fraction** if the numerator is less than the denominator. For example, $\frac{1}{2}, \frac{3}{5}$, and $\frac{8}{9}$ are all proper fractions.

A fraction is called an **improper fraction** if the numerator is greater than the denominator. For example, $\frac{4}{3}, \frac{5}{2}$, and $\frac{9}{8}$ are all improper fractions.

An improper fraction can alternatively be expressed as a **mixed number**, which includes an integer together with a proper fraction. For example, the mixed number $1\frac{1}{2}$ means one plus one-half, which is equivalent to the improper fraction $\frac{3}{2}$.

A mixed number, like $3\frac{1}{4}$, can be converted into an improper fraction. Multiply the denominator (in this case, 4) times the whole number (in this case, 3) and add the numerator (in this case, 1): $4 \times 3 + 1 = 13$. This is the numerator of the improper fraction. The improper fraction and mixed number have the same denominator. So $3\frac{1}{4}$ is equivalent to $\frac{13}{4}$. Following are a few more examples of this.

Examples converting mixed numbers into improper fractions:

$$4\frac{1}{2} = \frac{2 \times 4 + 1}{2} = \frac{9}{2}$$

$$5\frac{3}{8} = \frac{8 \times 5 + 3}{8} = \frac{43}{8}$$

$$2\frac{4}{5} = \frac{5 \times 2 + 4}{5} = \frac{14}{5}$$

To convert an improper fraction, like $\frac{13}{4}$, into a mixed number, divide the numerator (in this case, 13) by the denominator (in this case, 4). The result of the division – called the **quotient** – includes an integer part and a **remainder**. The integer part is the whole number of the mixed number and the remainder is the numerator. The mixed number has the same denominator. In this example, $13 \div 4 = 3R1$. That is, 13 divided by 4 equals 3 with a remainder of 1. Therefore, $\frac{13}{4}$ is equivalent to $3\frac{1}{4}$. Following are a few more examples of this.

Examples converting improper fractions into mixed numbers:

$$\frac{9}{2} = 9 \div 2 = 4R1 = 4\frac{1}{2}$$

$$\frac{14}{5} = 14 \div 5 = 2R4 = 2\frac{4}{5}$$

$$\frac{43}{8} = 43 \div 8 = 5R3 = 5\frac{3}{8}$$

When two or more numbers are multiplied together, the numbers being multiplied are called **factors**. For example, in $6 \times 2 = 12$, the 6 and 2 are called factors. Note that 12 can also be factored as $4 \times 3 = 12$. In this case, the 4 and 3 are factors. The **prime factors** of 12 are 2, 2, and 3 since $2 \times 2 \times 3 = 12$.

A pair of numbers, like 12 and 18, may share **common factors**. For example, 12 and 18 are both divisible by 3, so 3 is a common factor of 12 and 18. The **greatest common factor** of 12 and 18 is 6 because 6 is the largest number that evenly divides into both 12 and 18.

A fraction, like $\frac{12}{18}$, can be reduced when the numerator and denominator share a common factor. The **reduced fraction** is obtained by dividing both the numerator and denominator by the greatest common factor. The fraction $\frac{12}{18}$ is reduced by dividing 12 by 6 and dividing 18 by 6 (since 6 is the greatest common factor of 12 and 18). Therefore, $\frac{12}{18} = \frac{12 \div 6}{18 \div 6} = \frac{2}{3}$. Whenever you solve a math problem and obtain an answer that is a fraction, you should always express your answer as a reduced fraction. Following are a few more examples of reducing fractions.

Examples reducing fractions:

$$\frac{16}{12} = \frac{16 \div 4}{12 \div 4} = \frac{4}{3} \quad , \quad \frac{15}{25} = \frac{15 \div 5}{25 \div 5} = \frac{3}{5}$$

$$\frac{4}{24} = \frac{4 \div 4}{24 \div 4} = \frac{1}{6} \quad , \quad \frac{10}{5} = \frac{10 \div 5}{5 \div 5} = \frac{2}{1} = 2$$

# Adding Proper/Improper Fractions to Integers

**Procedure**: A proper or improper fraction, like $\frac{4}{3}$, can be added to an integer, like 2, to form a mixed number. In this case, $\frac{4}{3} + 2 = 2\frac{4}{3}$, which is an **improper mixed number**. The resulting mixed number, $2\frac{4}{3}$, can be converted into an improper fraction following the technique described on pages 5-6. In this case, $2\frac{4}{3}$ equates to $\frac{10}{3}$.

**Directions**: In this chapter, each problem consists of an integer plus a proper or improper fraction. Put these together to form a mixed number. Convert this mixed number into an improper fraction. Study the examples below before you begin.

## EXAMPLES

$$\frac{1}{3} + 2 = 2\frac{1}{3} = \frac{3 \times 2 + 1}{3} = \frac{7}{3}$$

$$3 + \frac{2}{5} = 3\frac{2}{5} = \frac{5 \times 3 + 2}{5} = \frac{17}{5}$$

$$\frac{9}{4} + 1 = 1\frac{9}{4} = \frac{4 \times 1 + 9}{4} = \frac{13}{4}$$

$$1 + \frac{3}{4} =$$

$$\frac{3}{7} + 9 =$$

$$8 + \frac{12}{7} =$$

$$\frac{5}{4} + 8 =$$

$$2 + \frac{4}{9} =$$

$$\frac{1}{8} + 5 =$$

$$3 + \frac{7}{8} =$$

$$\frac{7}{5} + 5 =$$

$$7 + \frac{1}{5} =$$

$$\frac{7}{5} + 9 =$$

$$8 + \frac{5}{4} =$$

$$\frac{2}{3} + 3 =$$

$$7 + \frac{1}{7} =$$

$$\frac{7}{3} + 1 =$$

$$5 + \frac{4}{9} =$$

$$\frac{5}{9} + 3 =$$

$$6 + \frac{1}{2} =$$

$$\frac{9}{5} + 7 =$$

$$4 + \frac{4}{9} =$$

$$\frac{7}{9} + 3 =$$

$$9 + \frac{9}{8} =$$

$$\frac{5}{9} + 7 =$$

$$4 + \frac{6}{5} =$$

$$\frac{11}{7} + 5 =$$

$$3 + \frac{11}{6} =$$

$$\frac{7}{8} + 6 =$$

$$9 + \frac{3}{5} =$$

$$\frac{7}{3} + 3 =$$

$$3 + \frac{9}{8} =$$

$$\frac{4}{5} + 9 =$$

$$7 + \frac{4}{9} =$$

$$\frac{7}{4} + 1 =$$

$$7 + \frac{1}{6} =$$

$$\frac{1}{2} + 8 =$$

$$3 + \frac{3}{7} =$$

$$\frac{10}{7} + 8 =$$

$$1 + \frac{2}{5} =$$

$$\frac{3}{7} + 1 =$$

$$5 + \frac{5}{6} =$$

$$\frac{7}{2} + 3 =$$

$$1 + \frac{1}{7} =$$

$$\frac{5}{7} + 8 =$$

$$7 + \frac{5}{9} =$$

$$\frac{2}{3} + 2 =$$

$$4 + \frac{7}{8} =$$

$$\frac{8}{3} + 8 =$$

$$2 + \frac{1}{7} =$$

$$\frac{5}{9} + 2 =$$

$$7 + \frac{7}{8} =$$

$$\frac{8}{9} + 3 =$$

$$6 + \frac{10}{7} =$$

$$\frac{2}{9} + 1 =$$

$$5 + \frac{2}{3} =$$

$$\frac{11}{6} + 7 =$$

$$8 + \frac{7}{8} =$$

$$\frac{3}{2} + 7 =$$

$$8 + \frac{8}{3} =$$

$$\frac{5}{2} + 5 =$$

$$5 + \frac{7}{2} =$$

$$\frac{2}{9} + 9 =$$

$$9 + \frac{4}{7} =$$

$$\frac{8}{9} + 2 =$$

$$9 + \frac{2}{9} =$$

$$\frac{7}{2} + 5 =$$

$$3 + \frac{7}{4} =$$

$$\frac{2}{3} + 5 =$$

$$4 + \frac{8}{9} =$$

$$\frac{6}{7} + 4 =$$

$$9 + \frac{4}{3} =$$

$$\frac{7}{4} + 7 =$$

$$1 + \frac{2}{7} =$$

$$\frac{1}{9} + 8 =$$

$$5 + \frac{9}{2} =$$

$$\frac{8}{9} + 7 =$$

$$9 + \frac{3}{7} =$$

$$\frac{1}{8} + 4 =$$

$$4 + \frac{5}{2} =$$

$$\frac{12}{7} + 9 =$$

$$7 + \frac{8}{7} =$$

$$\frac{3}{2} + 8 =$$

$$6 + \frac{5}{8} =$$

$$\frac{9}{4} + 4 =$$

$$7 + \frac{1}{2} =$$

$$\frac{1}{6} + 9 =$$

$$3 + \frac{9}{5} =$$

$$\frac{5}{9} + 9 =$$

$$2 + \frac{6}{7} =$$

$$\frac{13}{7} + 7 =$$

$$5 + \frac{7}{8} =$$

$$\frac{7}{5} + 1 =$$

$$6 + \frac{1}{9} =$$

$$\frac{7}{6} + 5 =$$

$$1 + \frac{9}{8} =$$

$$\frac{6}{5} + 8 =$$

$$4 + \frac{2}{7} =$$

$$\frac{8}{3} + 6 =$$

$$4 + \frac{5}{9} =$$

$$\frac{3}{8} + 3 =$$

$$6 + \frac{9}{7} =$$

$$\frac{3}{2} + 8 =$$

$$8 + \frac{5}{8} =$$

$$\frac{8}{9} + 7 =$$

$$9 + \frac{9}{8} =$$

$$\frac{6}{5} + 4 =$$

$$3 + \frac{11}{6} =$$

$$\frac{9}{5} + 3 =$$

$$5 + \frac{5}{2} =$$

$$\frac{1}{3} + 4 =$$

$$9 + \frac{7}{8} =$$

$$\frac{3}{8} + 3 =$$

$$8 + \frac{2}{3} =$$

$$\frac{1}{6} + 7 =$$

$$7 + \frac{4}{5} =$$

$$\frac{7}{4} + 6 =$$

$$1 + \frac{8}{7} =$$

$$\frac{2}{5} + 4 =$$

$$7 + \frac{7}{5} =$$

$$\frac{5}{9} + 9 =$$

$$2 + \frac{7}{4} =$$

$$\frac{7}{9} + 5 =$$

$$6 + \frac{5}{4} =$$

$$\frac{1}{9} + 1 =$$

$$8 + \frac{9}{8} =$$

$$\frac{5}{9} + 5 =$$

$$8 + \frac{7}{8} =$$

$$\frac{1}{3} + 9 =$$

$$6 + \frac{7}{9} =$$

$$\frac{5}{8} + 2 =$$

$$7 + \frac{7}{6} =$$

$$\frac{5}{6} + 6 =$$

$$3 + \frac{3}{4} =$$

$$\frac{1}{7} + 4 =$$

$$9 + \frac{4}{7} =$$

$$\frac{1}{9} + 8 =$$

$$1 + \frac{3}{7} =$$

$$\frac{11}{6} + 7 =$$

$$8 + \frac{1}{8} =$$

$$\frac{6}{5} + 6 =$$

$$8 + \frac{3}{2} =$$

$$\frac{12}{7} + 8 =$$

$$8 + \frac{7}{8} =$$

$$\frac{7}{4} + 1 =$$

$$2 + \frac{12}{7} =$$

$$\frac{3}{7} + 6 =$$

$$4 + \frac{5}{2} =$$

$$\frac{5}{4} + 2 =$$

$$7 + \frac{9}{4} =$$

$$\frac{1}{2} + 9 =$$

$$9 + \frac{6}{7} =$$

$$\frac{4}{9} + 3 =$$

$$7 + \frac{5}{7} =$$

$$\frac{2}{9} + 7 =$$

$$1 + \frac{3}{4} =$$

$$\frac{6}{7} + 3 =$$

$$2 + \frac{2}{5} =$$

$$\frac{1}{2} + 1 =$$

$$9 + \frac{1}{8} =$$

$$\frac{13}{7} + 5 =$$

$$2 + \frac{1}{5} =$$

$$\frac{1}{6} + 6 =$$

$$9 + \frac{3}{7} =$$

$$\frac{3}{8} + 5 =$$

$$3 + \frac{5}{6} =$$

$$\frac{5}{3} + 4 =$$

$$4 + \frac{9}{4} =$$

$$\frac{9}{5} + 9 =$$

$$4 + \frac{9}{8} =$$

$$\frac{9}{4} + 9 =$$

$$4 + \frac{6}{7} =$$

$$\frac{5}{9} + 4 =$$

$$3 + \frac{7}{4} =$$

$$\frac{1}{4} + 5 =$$

$$9 + \frac{1}{4} =$$

$$\frac{1}{7} + 4 =$$

$$9 + \frac{7}{2} =$$

$$\frac{6}{7} + 6 =$$

$$5 + \frac{5}{8} =$$

$$\frac{10}{7} + 6 =$$

$$8 + \frac{3}{5} =$$

$$\frac{1}{8} + 8 =$$

$$4 + \frac{9}{7} =$$

$$\frac{2}{7} + 1 =$$

$$6 + \frac{7}{8} =$$

$$\frac{3}{8} + 2 =$$

$3 + \dfrac{12}{7} =$

$\dfrac{8}{3} + 2 =$

$3 + \dfrac{7}{8} =$

$\dfrac{8}{5} + 3 =$

$2 + \dfrac{1}{8} =$

$\dfrac{1}{5} + 1 =$

$8 + \dfrac{7}{2} =$

$\dfrac{9}{2} + 3 =$

# Adding Two Proper/Improper Fractions Together

**Procedure**:  Proper or improper fractions, like $\frac{5}{6}$ and $\frac{7}{4}$, can be added together by first finding a **common denominator**.  A suitable common denominator can be found by multiplying the denominators together – in this case, that would be $6 \times 4 = 24$.  In order to convert each fraction to this common denominator, multiply each numerator by the other fraction's denominator.  Once you have a common denominator, you can add the numerators together.  For $\frac{5}{6} + \frac{7}{4}$, we get $\frac{5\times4}{6\times4} + \frac{7\times6}{4\times6} = \frac{20+42}{24} = \frac{62}{24}$, which reduces to $\frac{31}{12}$.  Note that $\frac{5\times4}{6\times4}$ equals $\frac{5}{6}$: If you multiply the numerator and denominator by the same factor, the fraction is unchanged (because any number divided by itself equals one).

**Directions**:  In this chapter, each problem consists of a sum of proper or improper fractions.  Follow the procedure outlined above.  Express your answer as an improper fraction.  Reduce your answer when possible (as described on page 7).  Study the examples on the next page before you begin.

## EXAMPLES

$$\frac{2}{3}+\frac{1}{4}=\frac{2\times 4}{3\times 4}+\frac{1\times 3}{4\times 3}=\frac{8+3}{12}=\frac{11}{12}$$

$$\frac{3}{4}+\frac{5}{2}=\frac{3\times 2}{4\times 2}+\frac{5\times 4}{2\times 4}=\frac{6+20}{8}=\frac{26}{8}=\frac{26\div 2}{8\div 2}=\frac{13}{4}$$

$$\frac{7}{3}+\frac{4}{9}=\frac{7\times 9}{3\times 9}+\frac{4\times 3}{9\times 3}=\frac{63+12}{27}=\frac{75}{27}=\frac{75\div 3}{27\div 3}=\frac{25}{9}$$

**Alternative Method.** It is convenient to find the **lowest common denominator**. The lowest common denominator is the smallest common multiple of the two denominators. For example, for $\frac{5}{6}$ and $\frac{7}{4}$, the lowest common denominator is 12, since 12 is the smallest number that is a multiple of both 6 and 4. Then multiply the numerator and denominator of each fraction by the factor needed to make the lowest common denominator. This is illustrated in the examples below.

## EXAMPLES

$$\frac{5}{6}+\frac{7}{4}=\frac{5\times 2}{6\times 2}+\frac{7\times 3}{4\times 3}=\frac{10+21}{12}=\frac{31}{12}$$

$$\frac{3}{4}+\frac{5}{2}=\frac{3\times 1}{4\times 1}+\frac{5\times 2}{2\times 2}=\frac{3+10}{4}=\frac{13}{4}$$

$$\frac{7}{3}+\frac{4}{9}=\frac{7\times 3}{3\times 3}+\frac{4\times 1}{9\times 1}=\frac{21+4}{9}=\frac{25}{9}$$

$$\frac{2}{9} + \frac{2}{3} =$$

$$\frac{12}{7} + \frac{8}{9} =$$

$$\frac{6}{5} + \frac{3}{8} =$$

$$\frac{5}{2} + \frac{3}{4} =$$

$$\frac{7}{5} + \frac{4}{7} =$$

$$\frac{8}{5} + \frac{2}{5} =$$

$$\frac{8}{3} + \frac{2}{9} =$$

$$\frac{7}{2} + \frac{5}{4} =$$

$$\frac{7}{2} + \frac{5}{6} =$$

$$\frac{5}{4} + \frac{11}{6} =$$

$$\frac{1}{2} + \frac{8}{3} =$$

$$\frac{2}{5} + \frac{5}{3} =$$

$$\frac{3}{4} + \frac{4}{3} =$$

$$\frac{1}{9} + \frac{5}{8} =$$

$$\frac{1}{4} + \frac{7}{9} =$$

$$\frac{5}{9} + \frac{9}{2} =$$

$$\frac{1}{3} + \frac{5}{3} =$$

$$\frac{9}{2} + \frac{7}{6} =$$

$$\frac{10}{7} + \frac{1}{6} =$$

$$\frac{4}{3} + \frac{3}{8} =$$

$$\frac{9}{2} + \frac{7}{9} =$$

$$\frac{10}{7} + \frac{8}{9} =$$

$$\frac{1}{9} + \frac{1}{9} =$$

$$\frac{8}{5} + \frac{2}{9} =$$

$$\frac{7}{9} + \frac{7}{6} =$$

$$\frac{7}{2} + \frac{8}{9} =$$

$$\frac{5}{2} + \frac{3}{7} =$$

$$\frac{9}{8} + \frac{7}{6} =$$

$$\frac{5}{7} + \frac{7}{3} =$$

$$\frac{9}{5} + \frac{3}{8} =$$

$$\frac{1}{2} + \frac{1}{9} =$$

$$\frac{2}{7} + \frac{8}{5} =$$

$$\frac{9}{2} + \frac{1}{6} =$$

$$\frac{9}{2} + \frac{1}{8} =$$

$$\frac{5}{9} + \frac{8}{7} =$$

$$\frac{5}{9} + \frac{7}{9} =$$

$$\frac{9}{4} + \frac{8}{3} =$$

$$\frac{7}{3} + \frac{9}{8} =$$

$$\frac{12}{7} + \frac{3}{5} =$$

$$\frac{5}{8} + \frac{7}{4} =$$

$$\frac{5}{6} + \frac{1}{9} =$$

$$\frac{7}{5} + \frac{8}{7} =$$

$$\frac{1}{2} + \frac{5}{6} =$$

$$\frac{9}{2} + \frac{7}{2} =$$

$$\frac{3}{4} + \frac{3}{2} =$$

$$\frac{7}{2} + \frac{7}{4} =$$

$$\frac{1}{8} + \frac{5}{8} =$$

$$\frac{7}{5} + \frac{4}{3} =$$

$$\frac{4}{5} + \frac{1}{5} =$$

$$\frac{5}{3} + \frac{3}{8} =$$

$$\frac{7}{6} + \frac{11}{6} =$$

$$\frac{7}{6} + \frac{2}{9} =$$

$$\frac{1}{7} + \frac{5}{4} =$$

$$\frac{5}{2} + \frac{1}{6} =$$

$$\frac{8}{5} + \frac{1}{2} =$$

$$\frac{3}{7} + \frac{1}{6} =$$

$$\frac{8}{3} + \frac{9}{4} =$$

$$\frac{3}{5} + \frac{5}{3} =$$

$$\frac{2}{3} + \frac{5}{2} =$$

$$\frac{5}{3} + \frac{11}{6} =$$

$$\frac{2}{3} + \frac{3}{8} =$$

$$\frac{9}{5} + \frac{1}{6} =$$

$$\frac{1}{5} + \frac{7}{8} =$$

$$\frac{2}{9} + \frac{4}{3} =$$

$$\frac{10}{7} + \frac{8}{3} =$$

$$\frac{7}{8} + \frac{7}{8} =$$

$$\frac{8}{9} + \frac{2}{5} =$$

$$\frac{11}{7} + \frac{2}{3} =$$

$$\frac{2}{7} + \frac{3}{5} =$$

$$\frac{9}{8} + \frac{11}{6} =$$

$$\frac{5}{4} + \frac{2}{7} =$$

$$\frac{8}{3} + \frac{4}{5} =$$

$$\frac{7}{6} + \frac{7}{9} =$$

$$\frac{5}{2} + \frac{5}{4} =$$

$$\frac{1}{3} + \frac{1}{2} =$$

$$\frac{5}{6} + \frac{13}{7} =$$

$$\frac{7}{8} + \frac{5}{6} =$$

$$\frac{7}{3} + \frac{2}{3} =$$

$$\frac{3}{8} + \frac{9}{7} =$$

$$\frac{13}{7} + \frac{1}{9} =$$

$$\frac{7}{8} + \frac{4}{9} =$$

$$\frac{2}{7} + \frac{11}{6} =$$

$$\frac{11}{6} + \frac{3}{4} =$$

$$\frac{5}{6} + \frac{3}{4} =$$

$$\frac{7}{8} + \frac{7}{3} =$$

$$\frac{5}{9} + \frac{1}{6} =$$

$$\frac{2}{9} + \frac{7}{6} =$$

$$\frac{9}{5} + \frac{8}{9} =$$

$$\frac{6}{5} + \frac{1}{8} =$$

$$\frac{8}{3} + \frac{2}{9} =$$

$$\frac{8}{9} + \frac{9}{5} =$$

$$\frac{5}{2} + \frac{11}{6} =$$

$$\frac{3}{2} + \frac{5}{9} =$$

$$\frac{1}{2} + \frac{3}{2} =$$

$$\frac{1}{5} + \frac{7}{4} =$$

$$\frac{2}{3} + \frac{4}{9} =$$

$$\frac{5}{6} + \frac{3}{8} =$$

$$\frac{6}{5} + \frac{11}{6} =$$

$$\frac{7}{6} + \frac{3}{7} =$$

$$\frac{9}{2} + \frac{9}{8} =$$

$$\frac{5}{3} + \frac{1}{4} =$$

$$\frac{7}{4} + \frac{1}{8} =$$

$$\frac{7}{9} + \frac{7}{5} =$$

$$\frac{7}{8} + \frac{1}{6} =$$

$$\frac{3}{8} + \frac{9}{4} =$$

$$\frac{7}{3} + \frac{3}{8} =$$

$$\frac{5}{6} + \frac{3}{2} =$$

$$\frac{5}{2} + \frac{7}{8} =$$

$$\frac{5}{4} + \frac{1}{2} =$$

$$\frac{2}{3} + \frac{3}{5} =$$

$$\frac{11}{6} + \frac{3}{4} =$$

$$\frac{1}{4} + \frac{4}{9} =$$

$$\frac{6}{5} + \frac{7}{8} =$$

$$\frac{9}{8} + \frac{1}{3} =$$

$$\frac{6}{5} + \frac{4}{5} =$$

$$\frac{7}{9} + \frac{7}{9} =$$

$$\frac{2}{9} + \frac{4}{3} =$$

$$\frac{11}{6} + \frac{2}{3} =$$

$$\frac{7}{6} + \frac{1}{9} =$$

$$\frac{10}{7} + \frac{1}{4} =$$

$$\frac{5}{6} + \frac{3}{4} =$$

$$\frac{3}{2} + \frac{4}{9} =$$

$$\frac{7}{9} + \frac{3}{5} =$$

$$\frac{3}{2} + \frac{5}{8} =$$

$$\frac{8}{9} + \frac{8}{5} =$$

$$\frac{9}{7} + \frac{9}{2} =$$

$$\frac{1}{3} + \frac{4}{7} =$$

$$\frac{5}{6} + \frac{5}{2} =$$

$$\frac{9}{5} + \frac{8}{3} =$$

$$\frac{3}{2} + \frac{5}{7} =$$

$$\frac{2}{5} + \frac{6}{7} =$$

$$\frac{4}{3} + \frac{5}{6} =$$

$$\frac{4}{3} + \frac{3}{8} =$$

$$\frac{8}{7} + \frac{9}{5} =$$

$$\frac{7}{9} + \frac{2}{3} =$$

$$\frac{3}{2} + \frac{7}{6} =$$

$$\frac{7}{8} + \frac{4}{7} =$$

$$\frac{7}{6} + \frac{8}{7} =$$

$$\frac{7}{2} + \frac{1}{8} =$$

$$\frac{8}{3} + \frac{7}{9} =$$

$$\frac{5}{3} + \frac{8}{3} =$$

$$\frac{9}{2} + \frac{5}{3} =$$

$$\frac{4}{9} + \frac{1}{8} =$$

$$\frac{4}{9} + \frac{9}{2} =$$

$$\frac{5}{6} + \frac{9}{2} =$$

$$\frac{9}{4} + \frac{7}{6} =$$

$$\frac{8}{9} + \frac{1}{3} =$$

$$\frac{9}{2} + \frac{5}{6} =$$

$$\frac{8}{3} + \frac{7}{3} =$$

$$\frac{4}{3} + \frac{1}{2} =$$

$$\frac{2}{9} + \frac{12}{7} =$$

$$\frac{8}{9} + \frac{5}{2} =$$

$$\frac{8}{9} + \frac{7}{5} =$$

$$\frac{6}{7} + \frac{9}{8} =$$

$$\frac{7}{9} + \frac{5}{3} =$$

$$\frac{2}{3} + \frac{9}{5} =$$

$$\frac{5}{6} + \frac{5}{2} =$$

$$\frac{11}{6} + \frac{11}{6} =$$

$$\frac{3}{4} + \frac{5}{4} =$$

$$\frac{9}{4} + \frac{5}{6} =$$

$$\frac{4}{3} + \frac{7}{8} =$$

$$\frac{1}{2} + \frac{7}{2} =$$

$$\frac{7}{5} + \frac{1}{6} =$$

$$\frac{7}{8} + \frac{9}{4} =$$

$$\frac{8}{5} + \frac{11}{6} =$$

$$\frac{9}{8} + \frac{5}{7} =$$

$$\frac{1}{6} + \frac{11}{6} =$$

$$\frac{7}{2} + \frac{5}{7} =$$

$$\frac{6}{5} + \frac{11}{6} =$$

$$\frac{3}{5} + \frac{11}{7} =$$

$$\frac{1}{5} + \frac{7}{4} =$$

$$\frac{9}{4} + \frac{3}{4} =$$

$$\frac{6}{5} + \frac{8}{3} =$$

$$\frac{4}{9} + \frac{4}{9} =$$

$$\frac{2}{5} + \frac{3}{5} =$$

$$\frac{7}{4} + \frac{9}{7} =$$

$$\frac{2}{3} + \frac{9}{5} =$$

$$\frac{7}{9} + \frac{7}{9} =$$

$$\frac{8}{7} + \frac{7}{3} =$$

$$\frac{5}{4} + \frac{11}{6} =$$

$$\frac{1}{8} + \frac{9}{5} =$$

$$\frac{7}{3} + \frac{8}{3} =$$

$$\frac{12}{7} + \frac{3}{2} =$$

$$\frac{3}{5} + \frac{8}{9} =$$

# Adding Two Mixed Numbers Together

**Procedure**: Two mixed numbers can be added together by first converting each mixed number into an improper fraction, as described on pages 5-6. Then add the improper fractions together, as described on pages 33-34.

**Directions**: In this chapter, each problem consists of a sum of mixed numbers. Follow the procedure outlined above. Reduce your answer when possible (as described on page 7). Express your answer as a mixed number. Study the examples below before you begin.

**EXAMPLES**

$$1\frac{2}{3} + 5\frac{1}{4} = \frac{3 \times 1 + 2}{3} + \frac{4 \times 5 + 1}{4} = \frac{5}{3} + \frac{21}{4}$$

$$= \frac{5 \times 4}{3 \times 4} + \frac{21 \times 3}{4 \times 3} = \frac{20 + 63}{12} = \frac{83}{12} = 6\frac{11}{12}$$

$$3\frac{1}{2} + 5\frac{4}{7} = \frac{2 \times 3 + 1}{2} + \frac{7 \times 5 + 4}{7} = \frac{7}{2} + \frac{39}{7}$$

$$= \frac{7 \times 7}{2 \times 7} + \frac{39 \times 2}{7 \times 2} = \frac{49 + 78}{14} = \frac{127}{14} = 9\frac{1}{14}$$

$$4\frac{1}{3} \;+\; 7\frac{1}{2} \;=$$

$$4\frac{3}{5} \;+\; 9\frac{1}{2} \;=$$

$$3\frac{3}{4} \;+\; 9\frac{3}{4} \;=$$

$$2\frac{4}{5} \;+\; 5\frac{2}{9} \;=$$

$$6\frac{1}{6} \;+\; 3\frac{3}{5} \;=$$

$$9\frac{5}{6} \;+\; 3\frac{5}{9} \;=$$

$$8\frac{3}{8} \;+\; 7\frac{1}{4} \;=$$

$$1\frac{1}{2} \;+\; 7\frac{1}{8} \;=$$

$$4 \frac{5}{7} + 9 \frac{1}{8} =$$

$$9 \frac{2}{3} + 5 \frac{5}{6} =$$

$$8 \frac{1}{2} + 1 \frac{1}{4} =$$

$$1 \frac{3}{5} + 8 \frac{1}{2} =$$

$$9 \frac{5}{6} + 5 \frac{5}{6} =$$

$$9 \frac{6}{7} + 5 \frac{3}{5} =$$

$$7 \frac{7}{8} + 9 \frac{2}{3} =$$

$$8 \frac{1}{3} + 9 \frac{1}{7} =$$

$1\dfrac{1}{2} \ + \ 2\dfrac{1}{2} =$

$9\dfrac{1}{2} \ + \ 2\dfrac{3}{8} =$

$2\dfrac{2}{9} \ + \ 8\dfrac{1}{3} =$

$1\dfrac{1}{2} \ + \ 9\dfrac{4}{5} =$

$4\dfrac{5}{6} \ + \ 2\dfrac{5}{7} =$

$3\dfrac{3}{4} \ + \ 2\dfrac{3}{4} =$

$4\dfrac{2}{3} \ + \ 6\dfrac{5}{7} =$

$1\dfrac{7}{9} \ + \ 8\dfrac{1}{6} =$

$$1 \frac{1}{6} \ + \ 6 \frac{4}{9} \ =$$

$$4 \frac{1}{4} \ + \ 2 \frac{1}{3} \ =$$

$$9 \frac{2}{3} \ + \ 2 \frac{2}{5} \ =$$

$$8 \frac{3}{4} \ + \ 3 \frac{2}{7} \ =$$

$$4 \frac{6}{7} \ + \ 3 \frac{7}{8} \ =$$

$$7 \frac{3}{8} \ + \ 8 \frac{1}{4} \ =$$

$$2 \frac{1}{4} \ + \ 1 \frac{5}{9} \ =$$

$$2 \frac{5}{6} \ + \ 1 \frac{3}{4} \ =$$

$3 \dfrac{5}{6} \ + \ 4 \dfrac{2}{3} =$

$9 \dfrac{5}{6} \ + \ 4 \dfrac{3}{4} =$

$5 \dfrac{2}{3} \ + \ 7 \dfrac{1}{2} =$

$6 \dfrac{2}{3} \ + \ 3 \dfrac{3}{8} =$

$9 \dfrac{1}{3} \ + \ 2 \dfrac{2}{5} =$

$1 \dfrac{2}{9} \ + \ 3 \dfrac{5}{7} =$

$4 \dfrac{1}{2} \ + \ 8 \dfrac{1}{2} =$

$3 \dfrac{1}{2} \ + \ 5 \dfrac{3}{8} =$

$5 \dfrac{5}{7} + 5 \dfrac{3}{7} =$

$1 \dfrac{1}{7} + 8 \dfrac{5}{6} =$

$7 \dfrac{1}{3} + 3 \dfrac{7}{8} =$

$7 \dfrac{5}{9} + 4 \dfrac{3}{8} =$

$8 \dfrac{1}{4} + 6 \dfrac{1}{3} =$

$4 \dfrac{1}{3} + 1 \dfrac{1}{2} =$

$1 \dfrac{1}{2} + 8 \dfrac{5}{7} =$

$7 \dfrac{1}{8} + 9 \dfrac{1}{3} =$

$3 \dfrac{1}{4} \ + \ 8 \dfrac{1}{3} =$

$1 \dfrac{5}{6} \ + \ 7 \dfrac{1}{2} =$

$4 \dfrac{3}{5} \ + \ 2 \dfrac{5}{8} =$

$5 \dfrac{1}{3} \ + \ 5 \dfrac{4}{9} =$

$1 \dfrac{4}{7} \ + \ 4 \dfrac{4}{9} =$

$6 \dfrac{1}{2} \ + \ 9 \dfrac{3}{4} =$

$6 \dfrac{3}{5} \ + \ 7 \dfrac{2}{7} =$

$1 \dfrac{1}{3} \ + \ 6 \dfrac{1}{4} =$

$$6 \frac{1}{8} \ + \ 9 \frac{2}{3} =$$

$$2 \frac{1}{7} \ + \ 8 \frac{1}{6} =$$

$$9 \frac{1}{2} \ + \ 7 \frac{5}{6} =$$

$$1 \frac{1}{4} \ + \ 7 \frac{1}{2} =$$

$$8 \frac{1}{7} \ + \ 8 \frac{3}{5} =$$

$$8 \frac{1}{8} \ + \ 3 \frac{3}{7} =$$

$$8 \frac{1}{2} \ + \ 6 \frac{1}{4} =$$

$$8 \frac{2}{5} \ + \ 9 \frac{3}{4} =$$

$4 \dfrac{1}{2} \ + \ 8 \dfrac{1}{4} =$

$3 \dfrac{6}{7} \ + \ 4 \dfrac{1}{2} =$

$5 \dfrac{1}{2} \ + \ 7 \dfrac{4}{7} =$

$2 \dfrac{4}{7} \ + \ 4 \dfrac{1}{2} =$

$7 \dfrac{1}{2} \ + \ 3 \dfrac{1}{5} =$

$8 \dfrac{2}{9} \ + \ 2 \dfrac{2}{3} =$

$5 \dfrac{4}{9} \ + \ 8 \dfrac{2}{3} =$

$3 \dfrac{7}{8} \ + \ 8 \dfrac{4}{9} =$

$8 \dfrac{5}{6} + 3 \dfrac{6}{7} =$

$5 \dfrac{1}{4} + 4 \dfrac{5}{6} =$

$8 \dfrac{3}{7} + 6 \dfrac{4}{9} =$

$2 \dfrac{3}{7} + 3 \dfrac{3}{5} =$

$4 \dfrac{2}{3} + 2 \dfrac{3}{5} =$

$8 \dfrac{1}{5} + 3 \dfrac{5}{6} =$

$3 \dfrac{4}{5} + 7 \dfrac{1}{6} =$

$4 \dfrac{5}{9} + 8 \dfrac{1}{3} =$

$$5 \frac{3}{4} + 8 \frac{2}{3} =$$

$$1 \frac{5}{8} + 7 \frac{1}{4} =$$

$$9 \frac{1}{8} + 2 \frac{5}{6} =$$

$$1 \frac{1}{7} + 8 \frac{2}{9} =$$

$$1 \frac{6}{7} + 5 \frac{1}{5} =$$

$$4 \frac{1}{2} + 4 \frac{1}{2} =$$

$$7 \frac{1}{2} + 5 \frac{4}{7} =$$

$$3 \frac{1}{6} + 6 \frac{5}{7} =$$

$$4\frac{1}{4} + 8\frac{1}{3} =$$

$$4\frac{5}{8} + 9\frac{3}{4} =$$

$$5\frac{7}{9} + 3\frac{2}{3} =$$

$$6\frac{7}{8} + 4\frac{1}{2} =$$

$$9\frac{3}{7} + 4\frac{1}{2} =$$

$$4\frac{1}{2} + 6\frac{1}{2} =$$

$$9\frac{8}{9} + 7\frac{1}{4} =$$

$$8\frac{2}{7} + 1\frac{1}{2} =$$

$$6 \frac{1}{9} \ + \ 6 \frac{2}{5} \ =$$

$$9 \frac{2}{5} \ + \ 8 \frac{1}{5} \ =$$

$$3 \frac{8}{9} \ + \ 2 \frac{4}{5} \ =$$

$$3 \frac{1}{8} \ + \ 2 \frac{1}{8} \ =$$

$$7 \frac{1}{2} \ + \ 1 \frac{2}{7} \ =$$

$$9 \frac{8}{9} \ + \ 4 \frac{1}{3} \ =$$

$$1 \frac{5}{7} \ + \ 4 \frac{4}{7} \ =$$

$$2 \frac{4}{5} \ + \ 6 \frac{1}{7} \ =$$

$$4 \frac{5}{9} + 8 \frac{5}{6} =$$

$$2 \frac{5}{6} + 2 \frac{1}{6} =$$

$$8 \frac{4}{5} + 2 \frac{1}{2} =$$

$$8 \frac{5}{6} + 2 \frac{2}{7} =$$

$$3 \frac{5}{6} + 7 \frac{7}{8} =$$

$$4 \frac{1}{4} + 5 \frac{1}{2} =$$

$$4 \frac{1}{2} + 6 \frac{1}{2} =$$

$$9 \frac{2}{3} + 2 \frac{1}{5} =$$

$$7\frac{6}{7} \ + \ 7\frac{2}{3} =$$

$$2\frac{1}{5} \ + \ 7\frac{3}{5} =$$

$$2\frac{3}{8} \ + \ 5\frac{1}{2} =$$

$$6\frac{7}{8} \ + \ 9\frac{4}{5} =$$

$$7\frac{4}{5} \ + \ 2\frac{1}{4} =$$

$$5\frac{2}{9} \ + \ 4\frac{2}{5} =$$

$$3\frac{1}{3} \ + \ 9\frac{2}{3} =$$

$$5\frac{1}{8} \ + \ 5\frac{4}{5} =$$

$$5 \frac{5}{8} + 7 \frac{3}{8} =$$

$$1 \frac{2}{3} + 3 \frac{1}{2} =$$

$$9 \frac{4}{5} + 2 \frac{3}{4} =$$

$$6 \frac{1}{4} + 7 \frac{1}{6} =$$

$$6 \frac{1}{4} + 6 \frac{3}{7} =$$

$$4 \frac{1}{4} + 6 \frac{2}{9} =$$

$$5 \frac{3}{4} + 1 \frac{3}{5} =$$

$$4 \frac{5}{7} + 5 \frac{5}{6} =$$

$$2\frac{2}{5} \;+\; 1\frac{3}{5} \;=$$

$$3\frac{1}{7} \;+\; 7\frac{3}{7} \;=$$

$$4\frac{8}{9} \;+\; 8\frac{1}{6} \;=$$

$$6\frac{6}{7} \;+\; 3\frac{3}{5} \;=$$

$$7\frac{2}{9} \;+\; 1\frac{1}{8} \;=$$

$$3\frac{3}{7} \;+\; 4\frac{4}{7} \;=$$

$$7\frac{3}{8} \;+\; 4\frac{3}{4} \;=$$

$$2\frac{1}{3} \;+\; 2\frac{4}{5} \;=$$

$$8 \frac{2}{5} + 1 \frac{2}{9} =$$

$$5 \frac{1}{2} + 3 \frac{1}{3} =$$

$$9 \frac{1}{7} + 9 \frac{3}{4} =$$

$$4 \frac{2}{5} + 7 \frac{2}{3} =$$

$$4 \frac{1}{8} + 9 \frac{1}{2} =$$

$$8 \frac{1}{2} + 8 \frac{3}{4} =$$

$$7 \frac{6}{7} + 1 \frac{1}{2} =$$

$$5 \frac{1}{3} + 8 \frac{2}{9} =$$

$$1\frac{3}{4} \ + \ 4\frac{7}{8} =$$

$$5\frac{1}{6} \ + \ 2\frac{5}{8} =$$

$$1\frac{1}{6} \ + \ 2\frac{3}{4} =$$

$$3\frac{2}{5} \ + \ 4\frac{1}{3} =$$

$$9\frac{2}{3} \ + \ 6\frac{1}{4} =$$

$$2\frac{5}{8} \ + \ 3\frac{5}{7} =$$

$$4\frac{6}{7} \ + \ 6\frac{1}{4} =$$

$$9\frac{1}{4} \ + \ 5\frac{1}{2} =$$

$$1\frac{1}{6} + 3\frac{4}{5} =$$

$$3\frac{1}{8} + 4\frac{2}{3} =$$

$$4\frac{7}{9} + 5\frac{2}{5} =$$

$$3\frac{2}{5} + 1\frac{4}{7} =$$

$$9\frac{4}{9} + 5\frac{1}{3} =$$

$$8\frac{4}{5} + 7\frac{2}{3} =$$

$$5\frac{1}{4} + 8\frac{1}{9} =$$

$$8\frac{5}{6} + 9\frac{3}{5} =$$

$$1 \frac{7}{8} \ + \ 8 \frac{4}{7} =$$

$$8 \frac{1}{4} \ + \ 7 \frac{4}{9} =$$

$$2 \frac{2}{3} \ + \ 7 \frac{1}{6} =$$

$$2 \frac{3}{7} \ + \ 7 \frac{3}{7} =$$

$$2 \frac{5}{6} \ + \ 2 \frac{1}{4} =$$

$$3 \frac{1}{2} \ + \ 6 \frac{3}{4} =$$

$$6 \frac{5}{6} \ + \ 2 \frac{1}{2} =$$

$$7 \frac{4}{7} \ + \ 7 \frac{1}{3} =$$

$2\dfrac{1}{2} + 6\dfrac{1}{2} =$

$3\dfrac{1}{2} + 6\dfrac{1}{4} =$

$5\dfrac{1}{2} + 6\dfrac{5}{9} =$

$4\dfrac{4}{5} + 6\dfrac{1}{6} =$

$3\dfrac{7}{8} + 2\dfrac{1}{8} =$

$8\dfrac{1}{8} + 9\dfrac{1}{2} =$

$2\dfrac{4}{5} + 8\dfrac{7}{8} =$

$4\dfrac{1}{6} + 2\dfrac{7}{8} =$

$6\dfrac{5}{7} \;+\; 6\dfrac{3}{8} =$

$3\dfrac{7}{8} \;+\; 7\dfrac{1}{6} =$

$6\dfrac{3}{5} \;+\; 9\dfrac{2}{3} =$

$2\dfrac{1}{2} \;+\; 5\dfrac{2}{5} =$

$6\dfrac{6}{7} \;+\; 7\dfrac{1}{3} =$

$3\dfrac{4}{5} \;+\; 1\dfrac{4}{7} =$

$5\dfrac{1}{2} \;+\; 2\dfrac{1}{7} =$

$9\dfrac{7}{9} \;+\; 4\dfrac{1}{6} =$

$3 \dfrac{5}{8} + 1 \dfrac{5}{8} =$

$5 \dfrac{1}{5} + 3 \dfrac{3}{7} =$

$7 \dfrac{1}{2} + 1 \dfrac{5}{8} =$

$3 \dfrac{3}{8} + 7 \dfrac{5}{8} =$

$4 \dfrac{8}{9} + 7 \dfrac{1}{4} =$

$8 \dfrac{7}{9} + 5 \dfrac{1}{8} =$

$5 \dfrac{3}{8} + 7 \dfrac{1}{2} =$

$5 \dfrac{5}{6} + 3 \dfrac{2}{7} =$

# Subtracting Proper/Improper Fractions to/from Integers

**Procedure**: When subtracting an integer from a proper or improper fraction – or when subtracting a proper or improper fraction from an integer – first write the integer as a fraction by dividing the integer by 1. Then multiply the integer and 1 both by the denominator of the fraction. This will give you a common denominator so that you can then subtract the numerators. For example, for $2 - \frac{5}{3}$, we write 2 as $\frac{2}{1}$ and then multiply both the 2 and 1 by 3: $\frac{2 \times 3}{1 \times 3} = \frac{6}{3}$. Then $\frac{6}{3} - \frac{5}{3} = \frac{1}{3}$.

**Directions**: In this chapter, each problem consists of subtraction between an integer and a proper or improper fraction. Follow the procedure outlined above to solve the problems. Express your answer as an improper fraction. Reduce your answer when possible (as described on page 7). Study the examples below before you begin.

## EXAMPLES

$$\frac{9}{4} - 2 = \frac{9}{4} - \frac{2}{1} = \frac{9}{4} - \frac{2 \times 4}{1 \times 4} = \frac{9 - 8}{4} = \frac{1}{4}$$

$$6 - \frac{2}{3} = \frac{6}{1} - \frac{2}{3} = \frac{6 \times 3}{1 \times 3} - \frac{2}{3} = \frac{18 - 2}{3} = \frac{16}{3}$$

$$\frac{9}{2} - 3 = \frac{9}{2} - \frac{3}{1} = \frac{9}{2} - \frac{3 \times 2}{1 \times 2} = \frac{9 - 6}{2} = \frac{3}{2}$$

$$3 - \frac{3}{2} =$$

$$8 - \frac{11}{6} =$$

$$\frac{51}{8} - 5 =$$

$$2 - \frac{8}{7} =$$

$$6 - \frac{11}{7} =$$

$$\frac{36}{5} - 2 =$$

$$5 - \frac{3}{5} =$$

$$4 - \frac{2}{9} =$$

$$\frac{11}{2} - 1 =$$

$$9 - \frac{2}{3} =$$

$$9 - \frac{9}{2} =$$

$$\frac{34}{5} - 4 =$$

$$6 - \frac{3}{5} =$$

$$6 - \frac{7}{9} =$$

$$\frac{23}{8} - 1 =$$

$$9 - \frac{2}{9} =$$

$$9 - \frac{5}{2} =$$

$$\frac{52}{9} - 1 =$$

$$1 - \frac{3}{4} =$$

$$9 - \frac{1}{5} =$$

$$\frac{41}{6} - 5 =$$

$$3 - \frac{3}{2} =$$

$$4 - \frac{3}{4} =$$

$$\frac{26}{5} - 3 =$$

$$4 - \frac{7}{2} =$$

$$4 - \frac{4}{7} =$$

$$\frac{10}{3} - 1 =$$

$$8 - \frac{3}{8} =$$

$$7 - \frac{1}{8} =$$

$$\frac{43}{5} - 4 =$$

$$5 - \frac{1}{6} =$$

$$7 - \frac{5}{3} =$$

$$\frac{7}{2} - 1 =$$

$$5 - \frac{7}{8} =$$

$$6 - \frac{6}{5} =$$

$$\frac{15}{7} - 1 =$$

$$5 - \frac{6}{7} =$$

$$6 - \frac{4}{3} =$$

$$\frac{8}{3} - 1 =$$

$$9 - \frac{6}{7} =$$

$7 - \dfrac{10}{7} =$

$\dfrac{14}{5} - 1 =$

$7 - \dfrac{9}{5} =$

$1 - \dfrac{1}{5} =$

$\dfrac{5}{2} - 1 =$

$6 - \dfrac{7}{5} =$

$3 - \dfrac{8}{3} =$

$\dfrac{22}{5} - 2 =$

$8 - \dfrac{7}{9} =$

$3 - \dfrac{11}{7} =$

$\dfrac{13}{6} - 1 =$

$4 - \dfrac{7}{3} =$

$6 - \dfrac{5}{7} =$

$\dfrac{10}{9} - 1 =$

$6 - \dfrac{7}{9} =$

$4 - \dfrac{9}{8} =$

$$\frac{19}{2} - 3 =$$

$$9 - \frac{5}{2} =$$

$$6 - \frac{4}{9} =$$

$$\frac{16}{5} - 1 =$$

$$3 - \frac{1}{9} =$$

$$4 - \frac{4}{9} =$$

$$\frac{4}{3} - 1 =$$

$$9 - \frac{5}{4} =$$

$$8 - \frac{7}{4} =$$

$$\frac{23}{7} - 1 =$$

$$6 - \frac{4}{3} =$$

$$6 - \frac{7}{2} =$$

$$\frac{25}{8} - 1 =$$

$$6 - \frac{7}{4} =$$

$$8 - \frac{1}{5} =$$

$$\frac{29}{4} - 3 =$$

$8 - \dfrac{5}{2} =$

$8 - \dfrac{5}{8} =$

$\dfrac{37}{5} - 3 =$

$8 - \dfrac{4}{7} =$

$8 - \dfrac{4}{9} =$

$\dfrac{16}{3} - 1 =$

$9 - \dfrac{8}{7} =$

$3 - \dfrac{8}{3} =$

$$\frac{16}{9} - 1 =$$

$$2 - \frac{7}{4} =$$

$$5 - \frac{11}{6} =$$

$$\frac{23}{3} - 2 =$$

$$9 - \frac{1}{2} =$$

$$6 - \frac{7}{5} =$$

$$\frac{37}{5} - 3 =$$

$$4 - \frac{7}{5} =$$

$$5 - \frac{7}{5} =$$

$$\frac{17}{2} - 6 =$$

$$3 - \frac{12}{7} =$$

$$4 - \frac{11}{7} =$$

$$\frac{36}{7} - 2 =$$

$$2 - \frac{1}{2} =$$

$$8 - \frac{7}{5} =$$

$$\frac{17}{8} - 1 =$$

$$2 - \frac{9}{8} =$$

$$2 - \frac{7}{4} =$$

$$\frac{13}{2} - 2 =$$

$$9 - \frac{7}{3} =$$

$$1 - \frac{2}{9} =$$

$$\frac{21}{4} - 4 =$$

$$7 - \frac{1}{3} =$$

$$6 - \frac{6}{5} =$$

$$\frac{83}{9} - 8 =$$

$$2 - \frac{1}{8} =$$

$$1 - \frac{7}{8} =$$

$$\frac{25}{6} - 3 =$$

$$4 - \frac{9}{5} =$$

$$9 - \frac{11}{7} =$$

$$\frac{14}{3} - 3 =$$

$$5 - \frac{5}{3} =$$

$$4 - \frac{4}{9} =$$

$$\frac{15}{2} - 2 =$$

$$5 - \frac{1}{9} =$$

$$4 - \frac{8}{9} =$$

$$\frac{59}{8} - 3 =$$

$$4 - \frac{5}{2} =$$

$$8 - \frac{8}{9} =$$

$$\frac{51}{7} - 4 =$$

$9 \ - \ \dfrac{9}{2} \ =$

$6 \ - \ \dfrac{5}{2} \ =$

$\dfrac{35}{4} \ - \ 2 \ =$

$3 \ - \ \dfrac{5}{7} \ =$

$8 \ - \ \dfrac{5}{2} \ =$

$\dfrac{29}{8} \ - \ 2 \ =$

$4 \ - \ \dfrac{3}{4} \ =$

$6 \ - \ \dfrac{7}{3} \ =$

$$\frac{27}{8} - 1 =$$

$$7 - \frac{2}{3} =$$

$$6 - \frac{1}{3} =$$

$$\frac{26}{5} - 2 =$$

$$4 - \frac{5}{3} =$$

$$9 - \frac{3}{8} =$$

$$\frac{8}{5} - 1 =$$

$$2 - \frac{1}{8} =$$

$$6 - \frac{3}{2} =$$

$$\frac{47}{5} - 7 =$$

$$9 - \frac{9}{4} =$$

$$6 - \frac{6}{7} =$$

$$\frac{16}{3} - 1 =$$

$$6 - \frac{1}{3} =$$

$$9 - \frac{5}{8} =$$

$$\frac{11}{8} - 1 =$$

$$4 - \frac{2}{9} =$$

$$9 - \frac{9}{2} =$$

$$\frac{22}{5} - 2 =$$

$$3 - \frac{7}{8} =$$

$$2 - \frac{2}{9} =$$

$$\frac{27}{4} - 2 =$$

$$7 - \frac{1}{2} =$$

$$5 - \frac{3}{4} =$$

$$\frac{14}{5} - 1 =$$

$$9 - \frac{5}{2} =$$

$$3 - \frac{3}{4} =$$

$$\frac{29}{6} - 2 =$$

$$3 - \frac{3}{5} =$$

$$4 - \frac{5}{6} =$$

$$\frac{27}{5} - 3 =$$

$$4 - \frac{7}{6} =$$

$$5 - \frac{3}{8} =$$

$$\frac{59}{6} - 1 =$$

$$5 - \frac{8}{9} =$$

$$9 - \frac{8}{9} =$$

$$\frac{5}{2} - 1 =$$

$$3 - \frac{2}{5} =$$

$$3 - \frac{1}{5} =$$

$$\frac{27}{4} - 5 =$$

$6 - \dfrac{8}{9} =$

$9 - \dfrac{1}{2} =$

$\dfrac{44}{5} - 3 =$

$2 - \dfrac{7}{4} =$

$6 - \dfrac{5}{6} =$

$\dfrac{33}{8} - 3 =$

$4 - \dfrac{4}{7} =$

$7 - \dfrac{9}{2} =$

$$\frac{17}{2} - 1 =$$

$$5 - \frac{3}{7} =$$

$$9 - \frac{11}{6} =$$

$$\frac{79}{9} - 7 =$$

$$5 - \frac{1}{6} =$$

$$8 - \frac{2}{3} =$$

$$\frac{23}{5} - 3 =$$

$$9 - \frac{5}{2} =$$

$$2 - \frac{7}{9} =$$

$$\frac{30}{7} - 1 =$$

$$7 - \frac{5}{4} =$$

$$5 - \frac{7}{6} =$$

$$\frac{31}{8} - 2 =$$

$$3 - \frac{1}{7} =$$

$$1 - \frac{3}{4} =$$

$$\frac{25}{8} - 2 =$$

# Subtracting Two Proper/Improper Fractions

**Procedure**: Subtract two proper/improper fractions with the same method that we used for adding them, except for subtracting the numerators after finding the common denominator. See pages 33-34. For example, for $\frac{7}{4} - \frac{5}{6}$, we get $\frac{7\times6}{4\times6} + \frac{5\times4}{6\times4} = \frac{42-20}{24} = \frac{22}{24}$, which reduces to $\frac{11}{12}$. Using the alternative method, the lowest common denominator is 12, and we get $\frac{7\times3}{4\times3} + \frac{5\times2}{6\times2} = \frac{21-10}{12} = \frac{11}{12}$.

**Directions**: In this chapter, each problem consists of proper or improper fractions subtracted from one another. Follow the procedure outlined above to solve the problems. Express your answer as an improper fraction. Reduce your answer when possible (as described on page 7). Study the examples below before you begin.

## EXAMPLES

$$\frac{2}{3} - \frac{1}{4} = \frac{2\times4}{3\times4} - \frac{1\times3}{4\times3} = \frac{8-3}{12} = \frac{5}{12}$$

$$\frac{5}{2} - \frac{3}{4} = \frac{5\times4}{2\times4} - \frac{3\times2}{4\times2} = \frac{20-6}{8} = \frac{14}{8} = \frac{14\div2}{8\div2} = \frac{7}{4}$$

$$\frac{7}{3} - \frac{4}{9} = \frac{7\times9}{3\times9} - \frac{4\times3}{9\times3} = \frac{63-12}{27} = \frac{51}{27} = \frac{51\div3}{27\div3} = \frac{17}{9}$$

$$\frac{12}{7} - \frac{4}{7} =$$

$$\frac{7}{4} - \frac{1}{2} =$$

$$\frac{9}{5} - \frac{5}{6} =$$

$$\frac{5}{2} - \frac{2}{5} =$$

$$\frac{3}{2} - \frac{6}{5} =$$

$$\frac{7}{3} - \frac{5}{9} =$$

$$\frac{11}{6} - \frac{11}{6} =$$

$$\frac{9}{8} - \frac{1}{3} =$$

$$\frac{9}{2} - \frac{4}{3} =$$

$$\frac{1}{6} - \frac{1}{9} =$$

$$\frac{9}{4} - \frac{1}{9} =$$

$$\frac{7}{4} - \frac{7}{5} =$$

$$\frac{3}{5} - \frac{1}{8} =$$

$$\frac{8}{3} - \frac{4}{5} =$$

$$\frac{1}{7} - \frac{1}{8} =$$

$$\frac{7}{3} - \frac{1}{2} =$$

$$\frac{5}{3} - \frac{1}{2} =$$

$$\frac{5}{4} - \frac{1}{6} =$$

$$\frac{3}{2} - \frac{10}{7} =$$

$$\frac{7}{8} - \frac{3}{7} =$$

$$\frac{5}{2} - \frac{7}{9} =$$

$$\frac{9}{4} - \frac{1}{8} =$$

$$\frac{9}{2} - \frac{3}{8} =$$

$$\frac{5}{9} - \frac{2}{9} =$$

$$\frac{3}{8} - \frac{1}{3} =$$

$$\frac{9}{4} - \frac{3}{8} =$$

$$\frac{7}{4} - \frac{3}{2} =$$

$$\frac{10}{7} - \frac{7}{8} =$$

$$\frac{5}{4} - \frac{5}{6} =$$

$$\frac{9}{2} - \frac{5}{9} =$$

$$\frac{3}{5} - \frac{1}{3} =$$

$$\frac{9}{2} - \frac{7}{9} =$$

$$\frac{7}{6} - \frac{1}{5} =$$

$$\frac{3}{4} - \frac{3}{8} =$$

$$\frac{3}{2} - \frac{1}{4} =$$

$$\frac{7}{4} - \frac{9}{8} =$$

$$\frac{5}{8} - \frac{1}{6} =$$

$$\frac{5}{4} - \frac{5}{6} =$$

$$\frac{8}{7} - \frac{2}{7} =$$

$$\frac{4}{7} - \frac{1}{8} =$$

$$\frac{5}{3} - \frac{1}{5} =$$

$$\frac{6}{5} - \frac{9}{8} =$$

$$\frac{5}{6} - \frac{2}{3} =$$

$$\frac{12}{7} - \frac{1}{4} =$$

$$\frac{7}{6} - \frac{1}{9} =$$

$$\frac{5}{4} - \frac{5}{4} =$$

$$\frac{4}{3} - \frac{9}{8} =$$

$$\frac{4}{3} - \frac{9}{8} =$$

$$\frac{9}{4} - \frac{3}{2} =$$

$$\frac{8}{9} - \frac{1}{3} =$$

$$\frac{5}{6} - \frac{5}{9} =$$

$$\frac{8}{5} - \frac{4}{9} =$$

$$\frac{7}{3} - \frac{4}{3} =$$

$$\frac{7}{8} - \frac{5}{9} =$$

$$\frac{11}{6} - \frac{1}{3} =$$

$$\frac{8}{9} - \frac{1}{9} =$$

$$\frac{3}{2} - \frac{1}{3} =$$

$$\frac{6}{7} - \frac{2}{5} =$$

$$\frac{7}{6} - \frac{7}{9} =$$

$$\frac{9}{5} - \frac{1}{3} =$$

$$\frac{7}{3} - \frac{5}{9} =$$

$$\frac{5}{2} - \frac{7}{9} =$$

$$\frac{11}{6} - \frac{6}{7} =$$

$$\frac{7}{2} - \frac{3}{5} =$$

$$\frac{9}{8} - \frac{5}{8} =$$

$$\frac{7}{4} - \frac{2}{3} =$$

$$\frac{7}{4} - \frac{7}{6} =$$

$$\frac{5}{9} - \frac{1}{6} =$$

$$\frac{3}{2} - \frac{5}{6} =$$

$$\frac{7}{3} - \frac{9}{4} =$$

$$\frac{8}{3} - \frac{8}{9} =$$

$$\frac{7}{6} - \frac{4}{9} =$$

$$\frac{4}{7} - \frac{4}{9} =$$

$$\frac{5}{8} - \frac{2}{9} =$$

$$\frac{7}{2} - \frac{3}{4} =$$

$$\frac{3}{4} - \frac{1}{2} =$$

$$\frac{5}{4} - \frac{3}{8} =$$

$$\frac{5}{2} - \frac{11}{6} =$$

$$\frac{5}{8} - \frac{3}{8} =$$

$$\frac{11}{6} - \frac{5}{6} =$$

$$\frac{2}{9} - \frac{1}{9} =$$

$$\frac{5}{2} - \frac{1}{2} =$$

$$\frac{4}{9} - \frac{1}{5} =$$

$$\frac{11}{7} - \frac{8}{9} =$$

$$\frac{9}{2} - \frac{11}{6} =$$

$$\frac{7}{4} - \frac{1}{8} =$$

$$\frac{7}{5} - \frac{4}{9} =$$

$$\frac{8}{9} - \frac{1}{9} =$$

$$\frac{7}{9} - \frac{4}{9} =$$

$$\frac{5}{2} - \frac{2}{7} =$$

$$\frac{2}{3} - \frac{5}{8} =$$

$$\frac{5}{7} - \frac{2}{3} =$$

$$\frac{3}{2} - \frac{4}{3} =$$

$$\frac{5}{8} - \frac{1}{2} =$$

$$\frac{11}{6} - \frac{7}{6} =$$

$$\frac{7}{5} - \frac{5}{9} =$$

$$\frac{5}{7} - \frac{5}{9} =$$

$$\frac{5}{6} - \frac{1}{4} =$$

$$\frac{5}{4} - \frac{4}{9} =$$

$$\frac{9}{4} - \frac{3}{8} =$$

$$\frac{6}{5} - \frac{7}{6} =$$

$$\frac{7}{2} - \frac{9}{8} =$$

$$\frac{1}{6} - \frac{1}{6} =$$

$$\frac{7}{5} - \frac{1}{6} =$$

$$\frac{1}{5} - \frac{1}{7} =$$

$$\frac{12}{7} - \frac{6}{7} =$$

$$\frac{5}{2} - \frac{4}{5} =$$

$$\frac{7}{4} - \frac{5}{9} =$$

$$\frac{5}{4} - \frac{8}{9} =$$

$$\frac{7}{2} - \frac{7}{4} =$$

$$\frac{7}{4} - \frac{2}{7} =$$

$$\frac{3}{2} - \frac{6}{7} =$$

$$\frac{5}{2} - \frac{8}{7} =$$

$$\frac{3}{4} - \frac{1}{2} =$$

$$\frac{11}{7} - \frac{2}{9} =$$

$$\frac{9}{5} - \frac{1}{4} =$$

$$\frac{12}{7} - \frac{1}{2} =$$

$$\frac{1}{3} - \frac{2}{9} =$$

$$\frac{7}{8} - \frac{5}{8} =$$

$$\frac{5}{2} - \frac{7}{4} =$$

$$\frac{3}{8} - \frac{1}{3} =$$

$$\frac{7}{3} - \frac{9}{8} =$$

$$\frac{7}{3} - \frac{1}{4} =$$

$$\frac{11}{7} - \frac{2}{3} =$$

$$\frac{5}{2} - \frac{9}{5} =$$

$$\frac{7}{3} - \frac{1}{3} =$$

$$\frac{7}{2} - \frac{11}{6} =$$

$$\frac{5}{4} - \frac{2}{5} =$$

$$\frac{5}{2} - \frac{8}{7} =$$

$$\frac{7}{6} - \frac{1}{4} =$$

$$\frac{5}{2} - \frac{8}{9} =$$

$$\frac{1}{5} - \frac{1}{6} =$$

$$\frac{7}{8} - \frac{2}{9} =$$

$$\frac{9}{2} - \frac{3}{5} =$$

$$\frac{5}{9} - \frac{4}{9} =$$

$$\frac{3}{8} - \frac{1}{4} =$$

$$\frac{7}{2} - \frac{7}{3} =$$

$$\frac{12}{7} - \frac{5}{4} =$$

$$\frac{9}{5} - \frac{1}{9} =$$

$$\frac{7}{8} - \frac{1}{2} =$$

$$\frac{7}{8} - \frac{5}{6} =$$

$$\frac{8}{7} - \frac{1}{2} =$$

$$\frac{3}{2} - \frac{7}{5} =$$

$$\frac{6}{5} - \frac{1}{8} =$$

$$\frac{7}{4} - \frac{1}{2} =$$

$$\frac{4}{3} - \frac{2}{5} =$$

$$\frac{9}{2} - \frac{1}{9} =$$

$$\frac{7}{6} - \frac{1}{6} =$$

$$\frac{5}{4} - \frac{7}{8} =$$

$$\frac{5}{8} - \frac{5}{9} =$$

$$\frac{11}{7} - \frac{2}{3} =$$

$$\frac{1}{3} - \frac{1}{8} =$$

Dr. Pi Squared Math Workbooks

$$\frac{7}{2} - \frac{5}{8} =$$

$$\frac{12}{7} - \frac{9}{7} =$$

$$\frac{5}{6} - \frac{1}{8} =$$

$$\frac{11}{6} - \frac{9}{7} =$$

$$\frac{9}{4} - \frac{7}{6} =$$

$$\frac{5}{6} - \frac{5}{7} =$$

$$\frac{5}{2} - \frac{7}{6} =$$

$$\frac{3}{2} - \frac{7}{9} =$$

$$\frac{3}{8} - \frac{1}{3} =$$

$$\frac{11}{7} - \frac{4}{7} =$$

$$\frac{10}{7} - \frac{5}{7} =$$

$$\frac{3}{4} - \frac{1}{3} =$$

$$\frac{9}{4} - \frac{10}{7} =$$

$$\frac{9}{8} - \frac{5}{9} =$$

$$\frac{2}{3} - \frac{4}{9} =$$

$$\frac{5}{8} - \frac{1}{5} =$$

$$\frac{5}{6} - \frac{5}{7} =$$

$$\frac{7}{4} - \frac{3}{2} =$$

$$\frac{9}{8} - \frac{7}{8} =$$

$$\frac{9}{5} - \frac{5}{6} =$$

$$\frac{7}{3} - \frac{1}{4} =$$

$$\frac{4}{3} - \frac{3}{8} =$$

$$\frac{5}{2} - \frac{1}{3} =$$

$$\frac{5}{3} - \frac{7}{6} =$$

$$\frac{2}{9} - \frac{1}{8} =$$

$$\frac{7}{2} - \frac{8}{3} =$$

$$\frac{5}{2} - \frac{7}{3} =$$

$$\frac{4}{9} - \frac{4}{9} =$$

$$\frac{5}{2} - \frac{4}{9} =$$

$$\frac{7}{4} - \frac{8}{9} =$$

$$\frac{9}{4} - \frac{10}{7} =$$

$$\frac{11}{7} - \frac{6}{5} =$$

$$\frac{9}{8} - \frac{1}{3} =$$

$$\frac{9}{2} - \frac{2}{9} =$$

$$\frac{9}{8} - \frac{1}{7} =$$

$$\frac{1}{3} - \frac{2}{9} =$$

$$\frac{8}{3} - \frac{3}{8} =$$

$$\frac{9}{4} - \frac{7}{4} =$$

$$\frac{7}{2} - \frac{1}{4} =$$

$$\frac{3}{2} - \frac{1}{9} =$$

# Subtracting Two Mixed Numbers

**Procedure**:  Subtract two mixed numbers with the same method that we used for adding them, except for subtracting the numerators after finding the common denominator after converting the mixed numbers to improper fractions.  See pages 33-34 and page 108.

**Directions**:   In this chapter, each problem consists of subtraction between two mixed numbers.  Follow the procedure outlined above to solve the problems.  Reduce your answer when possible (as described on page 7).  Express your answer as a mixed number.  Study the examples below before you begin.

**EXAMPLES**

$$5\frac{1}{4} - 1\frac{2}{3} = \frac{4 \times 5 + 1}{4} - \frac{3 \times 1 + 2}{3} = \frac{21}{4} - \frac{5}{3}$$

$$= \frac{21 \times 3}{4 \times 3} - \frac{5 \times 4}{3 \times 4} = \frac{63 - 20}{12} = \frac{43}{12} = 3\frac{7}{12}$$

$$5\frac{4}{7} - 3\frac{1}{2} = \frac{7 \times 5 + 4}{7} - \frac{2 \times 3 + 1}{2} = \frac{39}{7} - \frac{7}{2}$$

$$= \frac{39 \times 2}{7 \times 2} - \frac{7 \times 7}{2 \times 7} = \frac{78 - 49}{14} = \frac{29}{14} = 2\frac{1}{14}$$

$$8 \frac{2}{7} - 4 \frac{3}{8} =$$

$$6 \frac{2}{9} - 4 \frac{2}{3} =$$

$$5 \frac{1}{8} - 3 \frac{1}{4} =$$

$$5 \frac{1}{4} - 4 \frac{1}{4} =$$

$$9 \frac{3}{4} - 2 \frac{2}{5} =$$

$$9 \frac{1}{8} - 4 \frac{4}{9} =$$

$$9 \frac{7}{8} - 4 \frac{7}{9} =$$

$$7 \frac{2}{3} - 1 \frac{2}{3} =$$

$$8\frac{3}{4} - 7\frac{3}{4} =$$

$$5\frac{1}{2} - 2\frac{2}{3} =$$

$$3\frac{3}{4} - 2\frac{1}{2} =$$

$$8\frac{3}{4} - 2\frac{1}{7} =$$

$$6\frac{5}{9} - 4\frac{3}{4} =$$

$$8\frac{7}{8} - 8\frac{1}{2} =$$

$$7\frac{1}{2} - 3\frac{1}{3} =$$

$$9\frac{1}{4} - 6\frac{5}{6} =$$

$$6\frac{5}{8} - 6\frac{1}{9} =$$

$$9\frac{1}{3} - 3\frac{2}{3} =$$

$$7\frac{3}{5} - 5\frac{3}{7} =$$

$$8\frac{6}{7} - 6\frac{5}{6} =$$

$$7\frac{1}{6} - 2\frac{3}{4} =$$

$$5\frac{2}{7} - 3\frac{8}{9} =$$

$$2\frac{1}{9} - 1\frac{1}{2} =$$

$$9\frac{4}{7} - 6\frac{3}{4} =$$

$$5\frac{1}{2} - 3\frac{5}{9} =$$

$$9\frac{3}{5} - 9\frac{5}{9} =$$

$$9\frac{1}{4} - 1\frac{1}{3} =$$

$$3\frac{1}{7} - 1\frac{3}{4} =$$

$$8\frac{2}{3} - 4\frac{7}{8} =$$

$$2\frac{3}{5} - 1\frac{6}{7} =$$

$$9\frac{5}{8} - 1\frac{1}{7} =$$

$$9\frac{4}{9} - 1\frac{1}{2} =$$

$7\dfrac{3}{8}$ - $5\dfrac{1}{3}$ =

$8\dfrac{1}{5}$ - $7\dfrac{5}{8}$ =

$7\dfrac{2}{3}$ - $1\dfrac{1}{6}$ =

$7\dfrac{5}{7}$ - $3\dfrac{1}{5}$ =

$7\dfrac{1}{4}$ - $5\dfrac{1}{8}$ =

$9\dfrac{3}{8}$ - $6\dfrac{4}{5}$ =

$8\dfrac{1}{2}$ - $1\dfrac{5}{8}$ =

$5\dfrac{5}{8}$ - $3\dfrac{3}{5}$ =

$4 \dfrac{5}{6} - 4 \dfrac{5}{6} =$

$6 \dfrac{1}{8} - 5 \dfrac{1}{2} =$

$4 \dfrac{1}{2} - 1 \dfrac{1}{6} =$

$8 \dfrac{3}{4} - 8 \dfrac{4}{9} =$

$9 \dfrac{1}{4} - 1 \dfrac{3}{4} =$

$9 \dfrac{8}{9} - 5 \dfrac{1}{3} =$

$5 \dfrac{5}{6} - 4 \dfrac{4}{7} =$

$8 \dfrac{6}{7} - 4 \dfrac{1}{5} =$

$9 \dfrac{3}{7} - 7 \dfrac{1}{8} =$

$5 \dfrac{1}{8} - 1 \dfrac{3}{8} =$

$5 \dfrac{5}{9} - 1 \dfrac{2}{3} =$

$6 \dfrac{1}{4} - 3 \dfrac{3}{5} =$

$8 \dfrac{4}{5} - 7 \dfrac{1}{2} =$

$3 \dfrac{4}{7} - 3 \dfrac{4}{7} =$

$6 \dfrac{2}{3} - 2 \dfrac{8}{9} =$

$1 \dfrac{2}{5} - 1 \dfrac{2}{5} =$

$7 \dfrac{8}{9} - 4 \dfrac{6}{7} =$

$6 \dfrac{3}{4} - 6 \dfrac{2}{5} =$

$9 \dfrac{1}{4} - 1 \dfrac{1}{5} =$

$5 \dfrac{1}{5} - 4 \dfrac{2}{3} =$

$6 \dfrac{5}{9} - 1 \dfrac{7}{8} =$

$7 \dfrac{1}{2} - 4 \dfrac{1}{3} =$

$8 \dfrac{2}{3} - 3 \dfrac{7}{9} =$

$7 \dfrac{1}{2} - 5 \dfrac{1}{2} =$

$2\dfrac{1}{6} - 1\dfrac{2}{5} =$

$8\dfrac{2}{3} - 3\dfrac{7}{8} =$

$9\dfrac{2}{9} - 6\dfrac{1}{6} =$

$6\dfrac{5}{7} - 4\dfrac{5}{6} =$

$9\dfrac{1}{4} - 3\dfrac{1}{7} =$

$6\dfrac{5}{6} - 4\dfrac{5}{8} =$

$8\dfrac{1}{2} - 1\dfrac{1}{2} =$

$7\dfrac{1}{2} - 6\dfrac{1}{7} =$

$8 \dfrac{8}{9} - 4 \dfrac{1}{2} =$

$4 \dfrac{4}{5} - 2 \dfrac{2}{3} =$

$8 \dfrac{3}{4} - 7 \dfrac{3}{5} =$

$9 \dfrac{1}{9} - 1 \dfrac{3}{4} =$

$5 \dfrac{1}{8} - 2 \dfrac{6}{7} =$

$4 \dfrac{1}{5} - 1 \dfrac{1}{9} =$

$4 \dfrac{1}{2} - 2 \dfrac{1}{2} =$

$9 \dfrac{5}{8} - 2 \dfrac{1}{2} =$

$2\dfrac{1}{6} \; - \; 1\dfrac{6}{7} =$

$5\dfrac{2}{9} \; - \; 2\dfrac{4}{7} =$

$3\dfrac{3}{4} \; - \; 2\dfrac{2}{9} =$

$9\dfrac{1}{2} \; - \; 2\dfrac{5}{7} =$

$6\dfrac{1}{4} \; - \; 1\dfrac{1}{2} =$

$8\dfrac{1}{2} \; - \; 3\dfrac{2}{3} =$

$4\dfrac{3}{4} \; - \; 1\dfrac{1}{3} =$

$7\dfrac{1}{4} \; - \; 7\dfrac{1}{6} =$

$3 \dfrac{1}{8} \ - \ 1 \dfrac{3}{5} =$

$7 \dfrac{5}{6} \ - \ 3 \dfrac{3}{4} =$

$5 \dfrac{5}{9} \ - \ 2 \dfrac{1}{2} =$

$9 \dfrac{2}{3} \ - \ 4 \dfrac{1}{2} =$

$8 \dfrac{1}{2} \ - \ 8 \dfrac{2}{9} =$

$9 \dfrac{2}{5} \ - \ 3 \dfrac{2}{3} =$

$9 \dfrac{3}{4} \ - \ 5 \dfrac{3}{8} =$

$7 \dfrac{4}{7} \ - \ 2 \dfrac{1}{2} =$

$$9 \frac{1}{2} - 8 \frac{6}{7} =$$

$$4 \frac{5}{7} - 1 \frac{1}{4} =$$

$$6 \frac{1}{8} - 3 \frac{1}{3} =$$

$$2 \frac{3}{4} - 1 \frac{6}{7} =$$

$$7 \frac{3}{8} - 4 \frac{1}{2} =$$

$$7 \frac{5}{6} - 2 \frac{1}{4} =$$

$$8 \frac{1}{6} - 5 \frac{1}{2} =$$

$$5 \frac{1}{4} - 3 \frac{1}{7} =$$

$$9 \frac{2}{3} \; - \; 8 \frac{4}{7} =$$

$$8 \frac{1}{8} \; - \; 5 \frac{2}{5} =$$

$$6 \frac{7}{8} \; - \; 5 \frac{4}{7} =$$

$$2 \frac{1}{2} \; - \; 1 \frac{3}{7} =$$

$$7 \frac{3}{5} \; - \; 4 \frac{1}{8} =$$

$$7 \frac{3}{7} \; - \; 4 \frac{1}{4} =$$

$$6 \frac{1}{2} \; - \; 1 \frac{1}{5} =$$

$$9 \frac{3}{8} \; - \; 2 \frac{2}{7} =$$

$7 \dfrac{5}{8} \ - \ 4 \dfrac{1}{6} =$

$8 \dfrac{7}{9} \ - \ 4 \dfrac{1}{8} =$

$8 \dfrac{1}{6} \ - \ 7 \dfrac{3}{5} =$

$3 \dfrac{1}{2} \ - \ 1 \dfrac{5}{7} =$

$7 \dfrac{5}{7} \ - \ 5 \dfrac{1}{2} =$

$4 \dfrac{8}{9} \ - \ 3 \dfrac{5}{6} =$

$6 \dfrac{4}{5} \ - \ 5 \dfrac{1}{5} =$

$6 \dfrac{1}{2} \ - \ 4 \dfrac{3}{5} =$

$$9 \frac{3}{5} - 2 \frac{1}{2} =$$

$$5 \frac{4}{7} - 3 \frac{1}{6} =$$

$$3 \frac{3}{7} - 2 \frac{5}{7} =$$

$$5 \frac{5}{8} - 3 \frac{7}{8} =$$

$$8 \frac{1}{2} - 8 \frac{1}{2} =$$

$$8 \frac{2}{3} - 2 \frac{3}{7} =$$

$$5 \frac{4}{5} - 2 \frac{1}{9} =$$

$$9 \frac{5}{7} - 2 \frac{3}{5} =$$

$$8 \frac{7}{8} \ - \ 8 \frac{1}{2} =$$

$$3 \frac{5}{8} \ - \ 1 \frac{1}{6} =$$

$$4 \frac{3}{4} \ - \ 3 \frac{3}{7} =$$

$$3 \frac{4}{5} \ - \ 3 \frac{4}{5} =$$

$$9 \frac{4}{7} \ - \ 6 \frac{3}{4} =$$

$$9 \frac{1}{2} \ - \ 3 \frac{1}{8} =$$

$$5 \frac{1}{4} \ - \ 1 \frac{1}{4} =$$

$$5 \frac{1}{3} \ - \ 1 \frac{6}{7} =$$

$5 \dfrac{4}{9} - 3 \dfrac{1}{2} =$

$7 \dfrac{1}{7} - 5 \dfrac{1}{2} =$

$8 \dfrac{5}{8} - 6 \dfrac{5}{6} =$

$4 \dfrac{4}{9} - 2 \dfrac{3}{7} =$

$9 \dfrac{1}{3} - 5 \dfrac{1}{4} =$

$6 \dfrac{1}{9} - 5 \dfrac{1}{2} =$

$6 \dfrac{2}{5} - 4 \dfrac{1}{6} =$

$3 \dfrac{1}{2} - 3 \dfrac{1}{3} =$

$5 \dfrac{1}{2} \ - \ 2 \dfrac{1}{2} =$

$6 \dfrac{3}{5} \ - \ 5 \dfrac{3}{4} =$

$8 \dfrac{1}{8} \ - \ 4 \dfrac{7}{8} =$

$6 \dfrac{2}{3} \ - \ 4 \dfrac{1}{2} =$

$6 \dfrac{5}{6} \ - \ 4 \dfrac{6}{7} =$

$2 \dfrac{2}{9} \ - \ 1 \dfrac{2}{3} =$

$9 \dfrac{1}{5} \ - \ 5 \dfrac{1}{6} =$

$4 \dfrac{2}{7} \ - \ 3 \dfrac{2}{5} =$

$$8\frac{2}{9} - 2\frac{1}{5} =$$

$$6\frac{3}{4} - 6\frac{1}{3} =$$

$$8\frac{1}{8} - 5\frac{2}{3} =$$

$$7\frac{8}{9} - 2\frac{2}{3} =$$

$$7\frac{1}{2} - 1\frac{5}{8} =$$

$$9\frac{5}{9} - 4\frac{7}{8} =$$

$$9\frac{4}{5} - 3\frac{5}{6} =$$

$$5\frac{1}{3} - 2\frac{6}{7} =$$

$5\dfrac{5}{7} - 2\dfrac{1}{2} =$

$4\dfrac{2}{3} - 1\dfrac{4}{5} =$

$7\dfrac{6}{7} - 6\dfrac{1}{6} =$

$5\dfrac{8}{9} - 5\dfrac{7}{9} =$

$6\dfrac{3}{4} - 1\dfrac{3}{7} =$

$3\dfrac{1}{4} - 1\dfrac{8}{9} =$

$7\dfrac{5}{9} - 7\dfrac{1}{3} =$

$6\dfrac{3}{4} - 1\dfrac{1}{3} =$

$5 \dfrac{7}{8}$  -  $2 \dfrac{2}{9}$ =

$4 \dfrac{6}{7}$  -  $1 \dfrac{1}{6}$ =

$8 \dfrac{3}{8}$  -  $2 \dfrac{3}{4}$ =

$9 \dfrac{4}{7}$  -  $2 \dfrac{1}{3}$ =

$9 \dfrac{4}{5}$  -  $3 \dfrac{1}{2}$ =

$5 \dfrac{5}{9}$  -  $5 \dfrac{1}{8}$ =

$7 \dfrac{4}{5}$  -  $5 \dfrac{1}{3}$ =

$7 \dfrac{5}{8}$  -  $1 \dfrac{4}{9}$ =

$$6 \frac{3}{5} - 1 \frac{1}{2} =$$

$$3 \frac{2}{3} - 1 \frac{1}{5} =$$

$$2 \frac{5}{8} - 1 \frac{2}{3} =$$

$$4 \frac{4}{5} - 2 \frac{3}{7} =$$

$$9 \frac{8}{9} - 8 \frac{7}{8} =$$

$$8 \frac{5}{9} - 5 \frac{1}{3} =$$

$$4 \frac{1}{2} - 4 \frac{1}{6} =$$

$$6 \frac{6}{7} - 6 \frac{1}{2} =$$

$$8 \frac{5}{7} \quad - \quad 4 \frac{1}{2} =$$

$$6 \frac{1}{8} \quad - \quad 3 \frac{2}{5} =$$

$$3 \frac{1}{2} \quad - \quad 3 \frac{1}{8} =$$

$$7 \frac{2}{3} \quad - \quad 3 \frac{1}{6} =$$

$$5 \frac{5}{8} \quad - \quad 3 \frac{1}{4} =$$

$$3 \frac{1}{4} \quad - \quad 1 \frac{2}{3} =$$

$$7 \frac{3}{8} \quad - \quad 5 \frac{1}{8} =$$

$$6 \frac{1}{5} \quad - \quad 2 \frac{1}{8} =$$

# Answers

### Page 9

$$\frac{7}{4} \, , \, \frac{66}{7} \, , \, \frac{68}{7} \, , \, \frac{37}{4}$$

$$\frac{22}{9} \, , \, \frac{41}{8} \, , \, \frac{31}{8} \, , \, \frac{32}{5}$$

### Page 10

$$\frac{36}{5} \, , \, \frac{52}{5} \, , \, \frac{37}{4} \, , \, \frac{11}{3}$$

$$\frac{50}{7} \, , \, \frac{10}{3} \, , \, \frac{49}{9} \, , \, \frac{32}{9}$$

### Page 11

$$\frac{13}{2} \, , \, \frac{44}{5} \, , \, \frac{40}{9} \, , \, \frac{34}{9}$$

$$\frac{81}{8} \, , \, \frac{68}{9} \, , \, \frac{26}{5} \, , \, \frac{46}{7}$$

### Page 12

$$\frac{29}{6} \, , \, \frac{55}{8} \, , \, \frac{48}{5} \, , \, \frac{16}{3}$$

$$\frac{33}{8} \, , \, \frac{49}{5} \, , \, \frac{67}{9} \, , \, \frac{11}{4}$$

### Page 13

$$\frac{43}{6} \, , \, \frac{17}{2} \, , \, \frac{24}{7} \, , \, \frac{66}{7}$$

$$\frac{7}{5} \, , \, \frac{10}{7} \, , \, \frac{35}{6} \, , \, \frac{13}{2}$$

### Page 14

$$\frac{8}{7} \, , \, \frac{61}{7} \, , \, \frac{68}{9} \, , \, \frac{8}{3}$$

$$\frac{39}{8} \, , \, \frac{32}{3} \, , \, \frac{15}{7} \, , \, \frac{23}{9}$$

### Page 15

$$\frac{63}{8} \, , \, \frac{35}{9} \, , \, \frac{52}{7} \, , \, \frac{11}{9}$$

$$\frac{17}{3} \, , \, \frac{53}{6} \, , \, \frac{71}{8} \, , \, \frac{17}{2}$$

### Page 16

$$\frac{32}{3} \, , \, \frac{15}{2} \, , \, \frac{17}{2} \, , \, \frac{83}{9}$$

$$\frac{67}{7} \, , \, \frac{26}{9} \, , \, \frac{83}{9} \, , \, \frac{17}{2}$$

### Page 17

$$\frac{19}{4} \, , \, \frac{17}{3} \, , \, \frac{44}{9} \, , \, \frac{34}{7}$$

$$\frac{31}{3} \, , \, \frac{35}{4} \, , \, \frac{9}{7} \, , \, \frac{73}{9}$$

### Page 18

$$\frac{19}{2} \, , \, \frac{71}{9} \, , \, \frac{66}{7} \, , \, \frac{33}{8}$$

$$\frac{13}{2} \, , \, \frac{75}{7} \, , \, \frac{57}{7} \, , \, \frac{19}{2}$$

### Page 19

$$\frac{53}{8} \, , \, \frac{25}{4} \, , \, \frac{15}{2} \, , \, \frac{55}{6}$$

$$\frac{24}{5} \, , \, \frac{86}{9} \, , \, \frac{20}{7} \, , \, \frac{62}{7}$$

### Page 20

$$\frac{47}{8} \, , \, \frac{12}{5} \, , \, \frac{55}{9} \, , \, \frac{37}{6}$$

$$\frac{17}{8} \, , \, \frac{46}{5} \, , \, \frac{30}{7} \, , \, \frac{26}{3}$$

### Page 21

$$\frac{41}{9} , \frac{27}{8} , \frac{51}{7} , \frac{19}{2}$$

$$\frac{69}{8} , \frac{71}{9} , \frac{81}{8} , \frac{26}{5}$$

### Page 22

$$\frac{29}{6} , \frac{24}{5} , \frac{15}{2} , \frac{13}{3}$$

$$\frac{79}{8} , \frac{27}{8} , \frac{26}{3} , \frac{43}{6}$$

### Page 23

$$\frac{39}{5} , \frac{31}{4} , \frac{15}{7} , \frac{22}{5}$$

$$\frac{42}{5} , \frac{86}{9} , \frac{15}{4} , \frac{52}{9}$$

### Page 24

$$\frac{29}{4} , \frac{10}{9} , \frac{73}{8} , \frac{50}{9}$$

$$\frac{71}{8} , \frac{28}{3} , \frac{61}{9} , \frac{21}{8}$$

### Page 25

$$\frac{49}{6} , \frac{41}{6} , \frac{15}{4} , \frac{29}{7}$$

$$\frac{67}{7} , \frac{73}{9} , \frac{10}{7} , \frac{53}{6}$$

### Page 26

$$\frac{65}{8} , \frac{36}{5} , \frac{19}{2} , \frac{68}{7}$$

$$\frac{71}{8} , \frac{11}{4} , \frac{26}{7} , \frac{45}{7}$$

### Page 27

$$\frac{13}{2} , \frac{13}{4} , \frac{37}{4} , \frac{19}{2}$$

$$\frac{69}{7} , \frac{31}{9} , \frac{54}{7} , \frac{65}{9}$$

### Page 28

$$\frac{7}{4} , \frac{27}{7} , \frac{12}{5} , \frac{3}{2}$$

$$\frac{73}{8} , \frac{48}{7} , \frac{11}{5} , \frac{37}{6}$$

### Page 29

$$\frac{66}{7} , \frac{43}{8} , \frac{23}{6} , \frac{17}{3}$$

$$\frac{25}{4} , \frac{54}{5} , \frac{41}{8} , \frac{45}{4}$$

### Page 30

$$\frac{34}{7} , \frac{41}{9} , \frac{19}{4} , \frac{21}{4}$$

$$\frac{37}{4} , \frac{29}{7} , \frac{25}{2} , \frac{48}{7}$$

### Page 31

$$\frac{45}{8} , \frac{52}{7} , \frac{43}{5} , \frac{65}{8}$$

$$\frac{37}{7} , \frac{9}{7} , \frac{55}{8} , \frac{19}{8}$$

### Page 32

$$\frac{33}{7} , \frac{14}{3} , \frac{31}{8} , \frac{23}{5}$$

$$\frac{17}{8} , \frac{6}{5} , \frac{23}{2} , \frac{15}{2}$$

### Page 35
$$\frac{8}{9}, \quad \frac{164}{63}, \quad \frac{63}{40}, \quad \frac{13}{4}$$
$$\frac{69}{35}, \quad 2, \quad \frac{26}{9}, \quad \frac{19}{4}$$

### Page 36
$$\frac{13}{3}, \quad \frac{37}{12}, \quad \frac{19}{6}, \quad \frac{31}{15}$$
$$\frac{25}{12}, \quad \frac{53}{72}, \quad \frac{37}{36}, \quad \frac{91}{18}$$

### Page 37
$$2, \quad \frac{17}{3}, \quad \frac{67}{42}, \quad \frac{41}{24}$$
$$\frac{95}{18}, \quad \frac{146}{63}, \quad \frac{2}{9}, \quad \frac{82}{45}$$

### Page 38
$$\frac{35}{18}, \quad \frac{79}{18}, \quad \frac{41}{14}, \quad \frac{55}{24}$$
$$\frac{64}{21}, \quad \frac{87}{40}, \quad \frac{11}{18}, \quad \frac{66}{35}$$

### Page 39
$$\frac{14}{3}, \quad \frac{37}{8}, \quad \frac{107}{63}, \quad \frac{4}{3}$$
$$\frac{59}{12}, \quad \frac{83}{24}, \quad \frac{81}{35}, \quad \frac{19}{8}$$

### Page 40
$$\frac{17}{18}, \quad \frac{89}{35}, \quad \frac{4}{3}, \quad 8$$
$$\frac{9}{4}, \quad \frac{21}{4}, \quad \frac{3}{4}, \quad \frac{41}{15}$$

### Page 41
$$1, \quad \frac{49}{24}, \quad 3, \quad \frac{25}{18}$$
$$\frac{39}{28}, \quad \frac{8}{3}, \quad \frac{21}{10}, \quad \frac{25}{42}$$

### Page 42
$$\frac{59}{12}, \quad \frac{34}{15}, \quad \frac{19}{6}, \quad \frac{7}{2}$$
$$\frac{25}{24}, \quad \frac{59}{30}, \quad \frac{43}{40}, \quad \frac{14}{9}$$

### Page 43
$$\frac{86}{21}, \quad \frac{7}{4}, \quad \frac{58}{45}, \quad \frac{47}{21}$$
$$\frac{31}{35}, \quad \frac{71}{24}, \quad \frac{43}{28}, \quad \frac{52}{15}$$

### Page 44
$$\frac{35}{18}, \quad \frac{15}{4}, \quad \frac{5}{6}, \quad \frac{113}{42}$$
$$\frac{41}{24}, \quad 3, \quad \frac{93}{56}, \quad \frac{124}{63}$$

### Page 45
$$\frac{95}{72}, \quad \frac{89}{42}, \quad \frac{31}{12}, \quad \frac{19}{12}$$
$$\frac{77}{24}, \quad \frac{13}{18}, \quad \frac{25}{18}, \quad \frac{121}{45}$$

### Page 46
$$\frac{53}{40}, \quad \frac{26}{9}, \quad \frac{121}{45}, \quad \frac{13}{3}$$
$$\frac{37}{18}, \quad 2, \quad \frac{39}{20}, \quad \frac{10}{9}$$

### Page 47
$$\frac{29}{24}, \quad \frac{91}{30}, \quad \frac{67}{42}, \quad \frac{45}{8}$$
$$\frac{23}{12}, \quad \frac{15}{8}, \quad \frac{98}{45}, \quad \frac{25}{24}$$

### Page 48
$$\frac{21}{8}, \quad \frac{65}{24}, \quad \frac{7}{3}, \quad \frac{27}{8}$$
$$\frac{7}{4}, \quad \frac{19}{15}, \quad \frac{31}{12}, \quad \frac{25}{36}$$

### Page 49

$$\frac{83}{40} \ , \ \frac{35}{24} \ , \ 2 \ , \ \frac{14}{9}$$

$$\frac{14}{9} \ , \ \frac{5}{2} \ , \ \frac{23}{18} \ , \ \frac{47}{28}$$

### Page 50

$$\frac{19}{12} \ , \ \frac{35}{18} \ , \ \frac{62}{45} \ , \ \frac{17}{8}$$

$$\frac{112}{45} \ , \ \frac{81}{14} \ , \ \frac{19}{21} \ , \ \frac{10}{3}$$

### Page 51

$$\frac{67}{15} \ , \ \frac{31}{14} \ , \ \frac{44}{35} \ , \ \frac{13}{6}$$

$$\frac{41}{24} \ , \ \frac{103}{35} \ , \ \frac{13}{9} \ , \ \frac{8}{3}$$

### Page 52

$$\frac{81}{56} \ , \ \frac{97}{42} \ , \ \frac{29}{8} \ , \ \frac{31}{9}$$

$$\frac{13}{3} \ , \ \frac{37}{6} \ , \ \frac{41}{72} \ , \ \frac{89}{18}$$

### Page 53

$$\frac{16}{3} \ , \ \frac{41}{12} \ , \ \frac{11}{9} \ , \ \frac{16}{3}$$

$$5 \ , \ \frac{11}{6} \ , \ \frac{122}{63} \ , \ \frac{61}{18}$$

### Page 54

$$\frac{103}{45} \ , \ \frac{111}{56} \ , \ \frac{22}{9} \ , \ \frac{37}{15}$$

$$\frac{10}{3} \ , \ \frac{11}{3} \ , \ 2 \ , \ \frac{37}{12}$$

### Page 55

$$\frac{53}{24} \ , \ 4 \ , \ \frac{47}{30} \ , \ \frac{25}{8}$$

$$\frac{103}{30} \ , \ \frac{103}{56} \ , \ 2 \ , \ \frac{59}{14}$$

### Page 56

$$\frac{91}{30} \ , \ \frac{76}{35} \ , \ \frac{39}{20} \ , \ 3$$

$$\frac{58}{15} \ , \ \frac{8}{9} \ , \ 1 \ , \ \frac{85}{28}$$

### Page 57

$$\frac{37}{15} \ , \ \frac{14}{9} \ , \ \frac{73}{21} \ , \ \frac{37}{12}$$

$$\frac{77}{40} \ , \ 5 \ , \ \frac{45}{14} \ , \ \frac{67}{45}$$

### Page 59

$11 \dfrac{5}{6}$ , $14 \dfrac{1}{10}$ , $13 \dfrac{1}{2}$ , $8 \dfrac{1}{45}$

$9 \dfrac{23}{30}$ , $13 \dfrac{7}{18}$ , $15 \dfrac{5}{8}$ , $8 \dfrac{5}{8}$

### Page 60

$13 \dfrac{47}{56}$ , $15 \dfrac{1}{2}$ , $9 \dfrac{3}{4}$ , $10 \dfrac{1}{10}$

$15 \dfrac{2}{3}$ , $15 \dfrac{16}{35}$ , $17 \dfrac{13}{24}$ , $17 \dfrac{10}{21}$

### Page 61

$4$ , $11 \dfrac{7}{8}$ , $10 \dfrac{5}{9}$ , $11 \dfrac{3}{10}$

$7 \dfrac{23}{42}$ , $6 \dfrac{1}{2}$ , $11 \dfrac{8}{21}$ , $9 \dfrac{17}{18}$

### Page 62

$7 \dfrac{11}{18}$ , $6 \dfrac{7}{12}$ , $12 \dfrac{1}{15}$ , $12 \dfrac{1}{28}$

$8 \dfrac{41}{56}$ , $15 \dfrac{5}{8}$ , $3 \dfrac{29}{36}$ , $4 \dfrac{7}{12}$

### Page 63

$8 \dfrac{1}{2}$ , $14 \dfrac{7}{12}$ , $13 \dfrac{1}{6}$ , $10 \dfrac{1}{24}$

$11 \dfrac{11}{15}$ , $4 \dfrac{59}{63}$ , $13$ , $8 \dfrac{7}{8}$

### Page 64

$11 \dfrac{1}{7}$ , $9 \dfrac{41}{42}$ , $11 \dfrac{5}{24}$ , $11 \dfrac{67}{72}$

$14 \dfrac{7}{12}$ , $5 \dfrac{5}{6}$ , $10 \dfrac{3}{14}$ , $16 \dfrac{11}{24}$

Page 65

$11 \frac{7}{12}$ , $9 \frac{1}{3}$ , $7 \frac{9}{40}$ , $10 \frac{7}{9}$

$6 \frac{1}{63}$ , $16 \frac{1}{4}$ , $13 \frac{31}{35}$ , $7 \frac{7}{12}$

Page 66

$15 \frac{19}{24}$ , $10 \frac{13}{42}$ , $17 \frac{1}{3}$ , $8 \frac{3}{4}$

$16 \frac{26}{35}$ , $11 \frac{31}{56}$ , $14 \frac{3}{4}$ , $18 \frac{3}{20}$

Page 67

$12 \frac{3}{4}$ , $8 \frac{5}{14}$ , $13 \frac{1}{14}$ , $7 \frac{1}{14}$

$10 \frac{7}{10}$ , $10 \frac{8}{9}$ , $14 \frac{1}{9}$ , $12 \frac{23}{72}$

Page 68

$12 \frac{29}{42}$ , $10 \frac{1}{12}$ , $14 \frac{55}{63}$ , $6 \frac{1}{35}$

$7 \frac{4}{15}$ , $12 \frac{1}{30}$ , $10 \frac{29}{30}$ , $12 \frac{8}{9}$

Page 69

$14 \frac{5}{12}$ , $8 \frac{7}{8}$ , $11 \frac{23}{24}$ , $9 \frac{23}{63}$

$7 \frac{2}{35}$ , $9$ , $13 \frac{1}{14}$ , $9 \frac{37}{42}$

Page 70

$12 \frac{7}{12}$ , $14 \frac{3}{8}$ , $9 \frac{4}{9}$ , $11 \frac{3}{8}$

$13 \frac{13}{14}$ , $11$ , $17 \frac{5}{36}$ , $9 \frac{11}{14}$

Page 71

$12 \frac{23}{45}$ , $17 \frac{3}{5}$ , $6 \frac{31}{45}$ , $5 \frac{1}{4}$

$8 \frac{11}{14}$ , $14 \frac{2}{9}$ , $6 \frac{2}{7}$ , $8 \frac{33}{35}$

## Page 72

$13 \frac{7}{18}$ ,   $5$ ,   $11 \frac{3}{10}$ ,   $11 \frac{5}{42}$

$11 \frac{17}{24}$ ,   $9 \frac{3}{4}$ ,   $11$ ,   $11 \frac{13}{15}$

## Page 73

$15 \frac{11}{21}$ ,   $9 \frac{4}{5}$ ,   $7 \frac{7}{8}$ ,   $16 \frac{27}{40}$

$10 \frac{1}{20}$ ,   $9 \frac{28}{45}$ ,   $13$ ,   $10 \frac{37}{40}$

## Page 74

$13$ ,   $5 \frac{1}{6}$ ,   $12 \frac{11}{20}$ ,   $13 \frac{5}{12}$

$12 \frac{19}{28}$ ,   $10 \frac{17}{36}$ ,   $7 \frac{7}{20}$ ,   $10 \frac{23}{42}$

## Page 75

$4$ ,   $10 \frac{4}{7}$ ,   $13 \frac{1}{18}$ ,   $10 \frac{16}{35}$

$8 \frac{25}{72}$ ,   $8$ ,   $12 \frac{1}{8}$ ,   $5 \frac{2}{15}$

## Page 76

$9 \frac{28}{45}$ ,   $8 \frac{5}{6}$ ,   $18 \frac{25}{28}$ ,   $12 \frac{1}{15}$

$13 \frac{5}{8}$ ,   $17 \frac{1}{4}$ ,   $9 \frac{5}{14}$ ,   $13 \frac{5}{9}$

## Page 77

$6 \frac{5}{8}$ ,   $7 \frac{19}{24}$ ,   $3 \frac{11}{12}$ ,   $7 \frac{11}{15}$

$15 \frac{11}{12}$ ,   $6 \frac{19}{56}$ ,   $11 \frac{3}{28}$ ,   $14 \frac{3}{4}$

## Page 78

$4 \frac{29}{30}$ ,   $7 \frac{19}{24}$ ,   $10 \frac{8}{45}$ ,   $4 \frac{34}{35}$

$14 \frac{7}{9}$ ,   $16 \frac{7}{15}$ ,   $13 \frac{13}{36}$ ,   $18 \frac{13}{30}$

Page 79

$10 \frac{25}{56}$ , $15 \frac{25}{36}$ , $9 \frac{5}{6}$ , $9 \frac{6}{7}$

$5 \frac{1}{12}$ , $10 \frac{1}{4}$ , $9 \frac{1}{3}$ , $14 \frac{19}{21}$

Page 80

$9$ , $9 \frac{3}{4}$ , $12 \frac{1}{18}$ , $10 \frac{29}{30}$

$6$ , $17 \frac{5}{8}$ , $11 \frac{27}{40}$ , $7 \frac{1}{24}$

Page 81

$13 \frac{5}{56}$ , $11 \frac{1}{24}$ , $16 \frac{4}{15}$ , $7 \frac{9}{10}$

$14 \frac{4}{21}$ , $5 \frac{13}{35}$ , $7 \frac{9}{14}$ , $13 \frac{17}{18}$

Page 82

$5 \frac{1}{4}$ , $8 \frac{22}{35}$ , $9 \frac{1}{8}$ , $11$

$12 \frac{5}{36}$ , $13 \frac{65}{72}$ , $12 \frac{7}{8}$ , $9 \frac{5}{42}$

### Page 84

$$\frac{3}{2}, \frac{37}{6}, \frac{11}{8}, \frac{6}{7}$$

$$\frac{31}{7}, \frac{26}{5}, \frac{22}{5}, \frac{34}{9}$$

### Page 85

$$\frac{9}{2}, \frac{25}{3}, \frac{9}{2}, \frac{14}{5}$$

$$\frac{27}{5}, \frac{47}{9}, \frac{15}{8}, \frac{79}{9}$$

### Page 86

$$\frac{13}{2}, \frac{43}{9}, \frac{1}{4}, \frac{44}{5}$$

$$\frac{11}{6}, \frac{3}{2}, \frac{13}{4}, \frac{11}{5}$$

### Page 87

$$\frac{1}{2}, \frac{24}{7}, \frac{7}{3}, \frac{61}{8}$$

$$\frac{55}{8}, \frac{23}{5}, \frac{29}{6}, \frac{16}{3}$$

### Page 88

$$\frac{5}{2}, \frac{33}{8}, \frac{24}{5}, \frac{8}{7}$$

$$\frac{29}{7}, \frac{14}{3}, \frac{5}{3}, \frac{57}{7}$$

### Page 89

$$\frac{39}{7}, \frac{9}{5}, \frac{26}{5}, \frac{4}{5}$$

$$\frac{3}{2}, \frac{23}{5}, \frac{1}{3}, \frac{12}{5}$$

### Page 90

$$\frac{65}{9}, \frac{10}{7}, \frac{7}{6}, \frac{5}{3}$$

$$\frac{37}{7}, \frac{1}{9}, \frac{47}{9}, \frac{23}{8}$$

### Page 91

$$\frac{13}{2}, \frac{13}{2}, \frac{50}{9}, \frac{11}{5}$$

$$\frac{26}{9}, \frac{32}{9}, \frac{1}{3}, \frac{31}{4}$$

### Page 92

$$\frac{25}{4}, \frac{16}{7}, \frac{14}{3}, \frac{5}{2}$$

$$\frac{17}{8}, \frac{17}{4}, \frac{39}{5}, \frac{17}{4}$$

### Page 93

$$\frac{11}{2}, \frac{59}{8}, \frac{22}{5}, \frac{52}{7}$$

$$\frac{68}{9}, \frac{13}{3}, \frac{55}{7}, \frac{1}{3}$$

### Page 94

$$\frac{7}{9}, \frac{1}{4}, \frac{19}{6}, \frac{17}{3}$$

$$\frac{17}{2}, \frac{23}{5}, \frac{22}{5}, \frac{13}{5}$$

### Page 95

$$\frac{18}{5}, \frac{5}{2}, \frac{9}{7}, \frac{17}{7}$$

$$\frac{22}{7}, \frac{3}{2}, \frac{33}{5}, \frac{9}{8}$$

### Page 96

$$\frac{7}{8}, \frac{1}{4}, \frac{9}{2}, \frac{20}{3}$$

$$\frac{7}{9}, \frac{5}{4}, \frac{20}{3}, \frac{24}{5}$$

### Page 97

$$\frac{11}{9}, \frac{15}{8}, \frac{1}{8}, \frac{7}{6}$$

$$\frac{11}{5}, \frac{52}{7}, \frac{5}{3}, \frac{10}{3}$$

### Page 98

$$\frac{32}{9}, \frac{11}{2}, \frac{44}{9}, \frac{28}{9}$$

$$\frac{35}{8}, \frac{3}{2}, \frac{64}{9}, \frac{23}{7}$$

### Page 99

$$\frac{9}{2}, \frac{7}{2}, \frac{27}{4}, \frac{16}{7}$$

$$\frac{11}{2}, \frac{13}{8}, \frac{13}{4}, \frac{11}{3}$$

### Page 100

$$\frac{19}{8}, \frac{19}{3}, \frac{17}{3}, \frac{16}{5}$$

$$\frac{7}{3}, \frac{69}{8}, \frac{3}{5}, \frac{15}{8}$$

### Page 101

$$\frac{9}{2}, \frac{12}{5}, \frac{27}{4}, \frac{36}{7}$$

$$\frac{13}{3}, \frac{17}{3}, \frac{67}{8}, \frac{3}{8}$$

### Page 102

$$\frac{34}{9}, \frac{9}{2}, \frac{12}{5}, \frac{17}{8}$$

$$\frac{16}{9}, \frac{19}{4}, \frac{13}{2}, \frac{17}{4}$$

### Page 103

$$\frac{9}{5}, \frac{13}{2}, \frac{9}{4}, \frac{17}{6}$$

$$\frac{12}{5}, \frac{19}{6}, \frac{12}{5}, \frac{17}{6}$$

### Page 104

$$\frac{37}{8}, \frac{53}{6}, \frac{37}{9}, \frac{73}{9}$$

$$\frac{3}{2}, \frac{13}{5}, \frac{14}{5}, \frac{7}{4}$$

### Page 105

$$\frac{46}{9}, \frac{17}{2}, \frac{29}{5}, \frac{1}{4}$$

$$\frac{31}{6}, \frac{9}{8}, \frac{24}{7}, \frac{5}{2}$$

### Page 106

$$\frac{15}{2}, \frac{32}{7}, \frac{43}{6}, \frac{16}{9}$$

$$\frac{29}{6}, \frac{22}{3}, \frac{8}{5}, \frac{13}{2}$$

### Page 107

$$\frac{11}{9}, \frac{23}{7}, \frac{23}{4}, \frac{23}{6}$$

$$\frac{15}{8}, \frac{20}{7}, \frac{1}{4}, \frac{9}{8}$$

Dr. Pi Squared Math Workbooks

## Page 109

$$\frac{8}{7}, \frac{5}{4}, \frac{29}{30}, \frac{21}{10}$$

$$\frac{3}{10}, \frac{16}{9}, 0, \frac{19}{24}$$

## Page 110

$$\frac{19}{6}, \frac{1}{18}, \frac{77}{36}, \frac{7}{20}$$

$$\frac{19}{40}, \frac{28}{15}, \frac{1}{56}, \frac{11}{6}$$

## Page 111

$$\frac{7}{6}, \frac{13}{12}, \frac{1}{14}, \frac{25}{56}$$

$$\frac{31}{18}, \frac{17}{8}, \frac{33}{8}, \frac{1}{3}$$

## Page 112

$$\frac{1}{24}, \frac{15}{8}, \frac{1}{4}, \frac{31}{56}$$

$$\frac{5}{12}, \frac{71}{18}, \frac{4}{15}, \frac{67}{18}$$

## Page 113

$$\frac{29}{30}, \frac{3}{8}, \frac{5}{4}, \frac{5}{8}$$

$$\frac{11}{24}, \frac{5}{12}, \frac{6}{7}, \frac{25}{56}$$

## Page 114

$$\frac{22}{15}, \frac{3}{40}, \frac{1}{6}, \frac{41}{28}$$

$$\frac{19}{18}, 0, \frac{5}{24}, \frac{5}{24}$$

## Page 115

$$\frac{3}{4}, \frac{5}{9}, \frac{5}{18}, \frac{52}{45}$$

$$1, \frac{23}{72}, \frac{3}{2}, \frac{7}{9}$$

## Page 116

$$\frac{7}{6}, \frac{16}{35}, \frac{7}{18}, \frac{22}{15}$$

$$\frac{16}{9}, \frac{31}{18}, \frac{41}{42}, \frac{29}{10}$$

## Page 117

$$\frac{1}{2}, \frac{13}{12}, \frac{7}{12}, \frac{7}{18}$$

$$\frac{2}{3}, \frac{1}{12}, \frac{16}{9}, \frac{13}{18}$$

## Page 118

$$\frac{8}{63}, \frac{29}{72}, \frac{11}{4}, \frac{1}{4}$$

$$\frac{7}{8}, \frac{2}{3}, \frac{1}{4}, 1$$

## Page 119

$$\frac{1}{9}, 2, \frac{11}{45}, \frac{43}{63}$$

$$\frac{8}{3}, \frac{13}{8}, \frac{43}{45}, \frac{7}{9}$$

## Page 120

$$\frac{1}{3}, \frac{31}{14}, \frac{1}{24}, \frac{1}{21}$$

$$\frac{1}{6}, \frac{1}{8}, \frac{2}{3}, \frac{38}{45}$$

## Page 121

$$\frac{10}{63}, \frac{7}{12}, \frac{29}{36}, \frac{15}{8}$$

$$\frac{1}{30}, \frac{19}{8}, 0, \frac{37}{30}$$

## Page 122

$$\frac{2}{35}, \frac{6}{7}, \frac{17}{10}, \frac{43}{36}$$

$$\frac{13}{36}, \frac{7}{4}, \frac{41}{28}, \frac{9}{14}$$

## Page 123

$$\frac{19}{14}, \frac{1}{4}, \frac{85}{63}, \frac{31}{20}$$

$$\frac{17}{14}, \frac{1}{9}, \frac{1}{4}, \frac{3}{4}$$

## Page 124

$$\frac{1}{24}, \frac{29}{24}, \frac{25}{12}, \frac{19}{21}$$

$$\frac{7}{10}, 2, \frac{5}{3}, \frac{17}{20}$$

## Page 125

$$\frac{19}{14}, \frac{11}{12}, \frac{29}{18}, \frac{1}{30}$$

$$\frac{47}{72}, \frac{39}{10}, \frac{1}{9}, \frac{1}{8}$$

## Page 126

$$\frac{7}{6}, \frac{13}{28}, \frac{76}{45}, \frac{3}{8}$$

$$\frac{1}{24}, \frac{9}{14}, \frac{1}{10}, \frac{43}{40}$$

## Page 127

$$\frac{5}{4}, \frac{14}{15}, \frac{79}{18}, 1$$

$$\frac{3}{8}, \frac{5}{72}, \frac{19}{21}, \frac{5}{24}$$

## Page 128

$$\frac{23}{8}, \frac{3}{7}, \frac{17}{24}, \frac{23}{42}$$

$$\frac{13}{12}, \frac{5}{42}, \frac{4}{3}, \frac{13}{18}$$

## Page 129

$$\frac{1}{24}, 1, \frac{5}{7}, \frac{5}{12}$$

$$\frac{23}{28}, \frac{41}{72}, \frac{2}{9}, \frac{17}{40}$$

## Page 130

$$\frac{5}{42}, \frac{1}{4}, \frac{1}{4}, \frac{29}{30}$$

$$\frac{25}{12}, \frac{23}{24}, \frac{13}{6}, \frac{1}{2}$$

## Page 131

$$\frac{7}{72}, \frac{5}{6}, \frac{1}{6}, 0$$

$$\frac{37}{18}, \frac{31}{36}, \frac{23}{28}, \frac{13}{35}$$

## Page 132

$$\frac{19}{24}, \frac{77}{18}, \frac{55}{56}, \frac{1}{9}$$

$$\frac{55}{24}, \frac{1}{2}, \frac{13}{4}, \frac{25}{18}$$

### Page 134

$3\frac{51}{56}$ , $1\frac{5}{9}$ , $1\frac{7}{8}$ , $1$

$7\frac{7}{20}$ , $4\frac{49}{72}$ , $5\frac{7}{72}$ , $6$

### Page 135

$1$ , $2\frac{5}{6}$ , $1\frac{1}{4}$ , $6\frac{17}{28}$

$1\frac{29}{36}$ , $\frac{3}{8}$ , $4\frac{1}{6}$ , $2\frac{5}{12}$

### Page 136

$\frac{37}{72}$ , $5\frac{2}{3}$ , $2\frac{6}{35}$ , $2\frac{1}{42}$

$4\frac{5}{12}$ , $1\frac{25}{63}$ , $\frac{11}{18}$ , $2\frac{23}{28}$

### Page 137

$1\frac{17}{18}$ , $\frac{2}{45}$ , $7\frac{11}{12}$ , $1\frac{11}{28}$

$3\frac{19}{24}$ , $\frac{26}{35}$ , $8\frac{27}{56}$ , $7\frac{17}{18}$

### Page 138

$2\frac{1}{24}$ , $\frac{23}{40}$ , $6\frac{1}{2}$ , $4\frac{18}{35}$

$2\frac{1}{8}$ , $2\frac{23}{40}$ , $6\frac{7}{8}$ , $2\frac{1}{40}$

### Page 139

$0$ , $\frac{5}{8}$ , $3\frac{1}{3}$ , $\frac{11}{36}$

$7\frac{1}{2}$ , $4\frac{5}{9}$ , $1\frac{11}{42}$ , $4\frac{23}{35}$

### Page 140

$2\frac{17}{56}$ , $3\frac{3}{4}$ , $3\frac{8}{9}$ , $2\frac{13}{20}$

$1\frac{3}{10}$ , $0$ , $3\frac{7}{9}$ , $0$

### Page 141

$3 \frac{2}{63}$ , $\frac{7}{20}$ , $8 \frac{1}{20}$ , $\frac{8}{15}$

$4 \frac{49}{72}$ , $3 \frac{1}{6}$ , $4 \frac{8}{9}$ , $2$

### Page 142

$\frac{23}{30}$ , $4 \frac{19}{24}$ , $3 \frac{1}{18}$ , $1 \frac{37}{42}$

$6 \frac{3}{28}$ , $2 \frac{5}{24}$ , $7$ , $1 \frac{5}{14}$

### Page 143

$4 \frac{7}{18}$ , $2 \frac{2}{15}$ , $1 \frac{3}{20}$ , $7 \frac{13}{36}$

$2 \frac{15}{56}$ , $3 \frac{4}{45}$ , $2$ , $7 \frac{1}{8}$

### Page 144

$\frac{13}{42}$ , $2 \frac{41}{63}$ , $1 \frac{19}{36}$ , $6 \frac{11}{14}$

$4 \frac{3}{4}$ , $4 \frac{5}{6}$ , $3 \frac{5}{12}$ , $\frac{1}{12}$

### Page 145

$1 \frac{21}{40}$ , $4 \frac{1}{12}$ , $3 \frac{1}{18}$ , $5 \frac{1}{6}$

$\frac{5}{18}$ , $5 \frac{11}{15}$ , $4 \frac{3}{8}$ , $5 \frac{1}{14}$

### Page 146

$\frac{9}{14}$ , $3 \frac{13}{28}$ , $2 \frac{19}{24}$ , $\frac{25}{28}$

$2 \frac{7}{8}$ , $5 \frac{7}{12}$ , $2 \frac{2}{3}$ , $2 \frac{3}{28}$

### Page 147

$1 \frac{2}{21}$ , $2 \frac{29}{40}$ , $1 \frac{17}{56}$ , $1 \frac{1}{14}$

$3 \frac{19}{40}$ , $3 \frac{5}{28}$ , $5 \frac{3}{10}$ , $7 \frac{5}{56}$

### Page 148

$3\frac{11}{24}$ , $4\frac{47}{72}$ , $\frac{17}{30}$ , $1\frac{11}{14}$

$2\frac{3}{14}$ , $1\frac{1}{18}$ , $1\frac{3}{5}$ , $1\frac{9}{10}$

### Page 149

$7\frac{1}{10}$ , $2\frac{17}{42}$ , $\frac{5}{7}$ , $1\frac{3}{4}$

$0$ , $6\frac{5}{21}$ , $3\frac{31}{45}$ , $7\frac{4}{35}$

### Page 150

$\frac{3}{8}$ , $2\frac{11}{24}$ , $1\frac{9}{28}$ , $0$

$2\frac{23}{28}$ , $6\frac{3}{8}$ , $4$ , $3\frac{10}{21}$

### Page 151

$1\frac{17}{18}$ , $1\frac{9}{14}$ , $1\frac{19}{24}$ , $2\frac{1}{63}$

$4\frac{1}{12}$ , $\frac{11}{18}$ , $2\frac{7}{30}$ , $\frac{1}{6}$

### Page 152

$3$ , $\frac{17}{20}$ , $3\frac{1}{4}$ , $2\frac{1}{6}$

$1\frac{41}{42}$ , $\frac{5}{9}$ , $4\frac{1}{30}$ , $\frac{31}{35}$

### Page 153

$6\frac{1}{45}$ , $\frac{5}{12}$ , $2\frac{11}{24}$ , $5\frac{2}{9}$

$5\frac{7}{8}$ , $4\frac{49}{72}$ , $5\frac{29}{30}$ , $2\frac{10}{21}$

### Page 154

$3\frac{3}{14}$ , $2\frac{13}{15}$ , $1\frac{29}{42}$ , $\frac{1}{9}$

$5\frac{9}{28}$ , $1\frac{13}{36}$ , $\frac{2}{9}$ , $5\frac{5}{12}$

Page 155

$3 \frac{47}{72}$ , $3 \frac{29}{42}$ , $5 \frac{5}{8}$ , $7 \frac{5}{21}$

$6 \frac{3}{10}$ , $\frac{31}{72}$ , $2 \frac{7}{15}$ , $6 \frac{13}{72}$

Page 156

$5 \frac{1}{10}$ , $2 \frac{7}{15}$ , $\frac{23}{24}$ , $2 \frac{13}{35}$

$1 \frac{1}{72}$ , $3 \frac{2}{9}$ , $\frac{1}{3}$ , $\frac{5}{14}$

Page 157

$4 \frac{3}{14}$ , $2 \frac{29}{40}$ , $\frac{3}{8}$ , $4 \frac{1}{2}$

$2 \frac{3}{8}$ , $1 \frac{7}{12}$ , $2 \frac{1}{4}$ , $4 \frac{3}{40}$

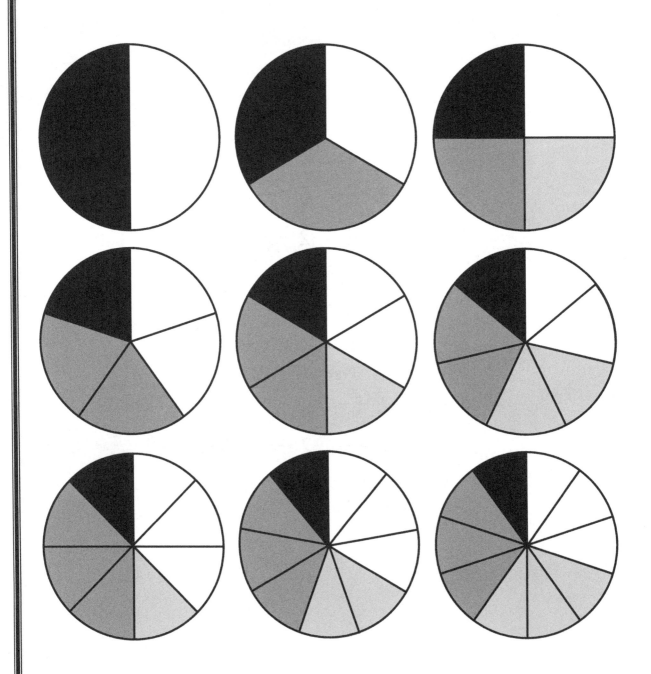

Made in United States
Orlando, FL
02 August 2024

49837289R00096